DIY QuickBooks Online for Beginners

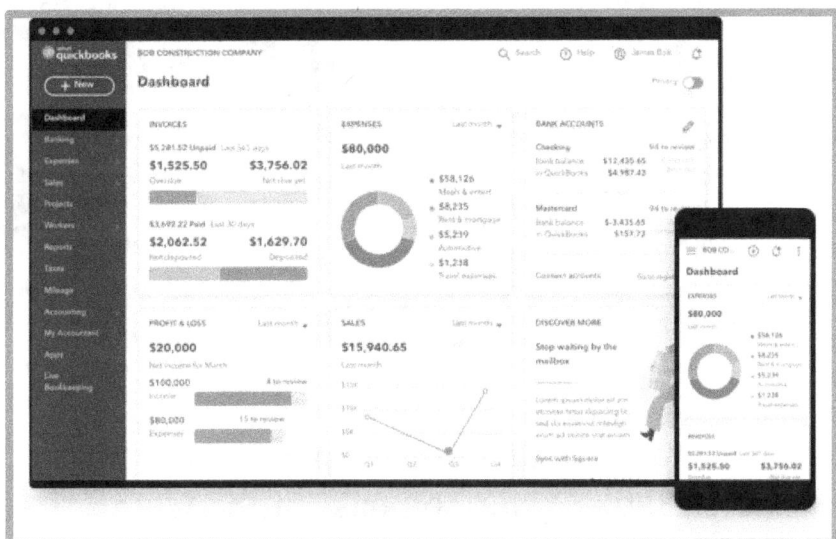

Robert Lewis

BOOKKEEPING MADE EASY

Unlock the power of financial control and pave your path to prosperity. Embrace QuickBooks, your compass in the world of business. Learning is your key to success; let QuickBooks for Beginners be your guiding light.

Become an up-to-date accountant and bookkeeper

Table of contents

KEEP TRACK OF YOUR FINANCES

INTRODUCTION

Navigating the financial landscape can be a daunting task, and for bookkeepers and accountants who aren't well-versed in using QuickBooks Online, the challenges can be even more overwhelming. QuickBooks Online is a powerful tool, but mastering it is crucial for professionals in the finance industry.

One of the primary challenges faced by bookkeepers and accountants unfamiliar with QuickBooks Online is inefficiency. Manual bookkeeping and traditional accounting methods are not only time-consuming but also prone to errors. Without a solid understanding of QuickBooks Online, these professionals miss out on the automation, accuracy, and time-saving features it offers.

Data security is another significant concern. QuickBooks Online is a cloud-based platform, and without the knowledge to set up robust security measures, sensitive financial data could be at risk. Bookkeepers and accountants must grasp the importance of data protection and privacy within the online environment to ensure their clients' information remains safe.

Furthermore, without a strong command of QuickBooks Online, professionals may find themselves struggling to provide real-time insights to their clients. The platform's reporting and analytics capabilities can be a game-changer, allowing accountants to offer valuable advice and forecasts. However, lacking these skills can result in delayed or inaccurate financial insights.

Another challenge lies in missed opportunities. QuickBooks Online facilitates the management of business finances and offers a variety of features that can benefit clients. Bookkeepers and accountants need to understand these capabilities to provide comprehensive support. Not leveraging the full potential of the platform can result in lost opportunities for client growth and satisfaction.

The challenges faced by bookkeepers and accountants who lack proficiency in QuickBooks Online are multifaceted. They encompass issues of efficiency, data security, real-time reporting, and maximizing the potential of the platform for their clients. Overcoming these challenges requires a commitment to learning and adapting to the evolving landscape of financial management.

Step into the world of QuickBooks, where innovation meets business. Developed and marketed by Intuit, QuickBooks has been a game-changer for small and medium-sized enterprises since its inception in 1983.

This is the story of how a company founded by Scott Cook and Tom Proulx in the heart of Mountain View, California, revolutionized financial management and accounting for entrepreneurs.

Starting with the immense success of Quicken, their personal financial management software, Intuit saw the potential to serve a broader clientele. The result was QuickBooks, a powerful accounting solution that found its roots in the Quicken codebase, paving the way for its first DOS version. As the Windows and Mac versions took shape, Intuit's acquisition of In-House Accountant enriched the software's foundation

QuickBooks quickly gained popularity among small business owners who sought a user-friendly accounting tool. It captured a whopping 85% of the market for small business accounting software in the US, a dominance it still maintained in 2013.

However, the software's early versions faced criticism from professional accountants for lacking essential features like a comprehensive audit trail and compliance with conventional accounting standards

With the introduction of QuickBooks Online, Intuit transformed the game. This cloud-based service shifted from traditional one-time pricing to a convenient monthly subscription model.

Users could access their accounts securely through a web browser, benefit from regular updates, and support from Intuit. Yet, the innovation came with the trade-off of occasional pop-up advertisements for premium services.

QuickBooks Online, as of May 2014, led the race with 624,000 subscribers, leaving competitors like Xero far behind.

The cloud version of QuickBooks is not just a replica of its desktop counterpart. It offers unique features, including customization options and third-party integration. In 2013, Intuit declared a ground-up rebuild of QuickBooks Online, allowing users to tailor their experience and fostering a community of small business application developers.

This is the journey of QuickBooks – an evolution that shaped the landscape of financial management for businesses across the globe.

Embrace the QuickBooks journey with determination. In every challenge, see an opportunity to become a financial virtuoso. With each task mastered, you edge closer to financial excellence. Let the desire for knowledge and skill fuel your QuickBooks learning, for in this realm, the determined thrive. The path to financial competence may be winding, but every twist and turn equips you with invaluable expertise. Remember, great accountants and bookkeepers are not born; they are made through dedication.

CHAPTER 1

UNVEILING QUICKBOOKS ONLINE

QuickBooks Online: A Glimpse

Enter the realm of QuickBooks Online, a revolutionary cloud-based accounting solution tailored to empower small businesses. Within this digital ecosystem, businesses harness the power of online access to streamline their financial operations, from accounting and income management to expenditure control and seamless payroll processing.

Dive into the world of online financial management, where all your accounts reside in a virtual interface. This modern landscape is adorned with features like custom feeds, interactive charts, invoice customization, 'Pay Now' functionality, and mobile optimization, seamlessly synchronized to deliver unparalleled financial efficiency.

Mobile Empowerment

Embark on your QuickBooks Online journey with the convenience of dedicated mobile apps, available on both Android and iOS platforms. These apps become your companions in financial management, enabling swift capture of sales receipts, real-time expense monitoring, vigilant cash flow management, constant account balance tracking, precise time tracking, in-depth transaction reviews, efficient purchase order management, seamless client communications, and much more. QuickBooks Online's mobile apps redefine financial mobility, putting the power of comprehensive financial control right in the palm of your hand.

Unified Financial Insights

Experience the magic of synergy as QuickBooks Online automatically syncs your business finance profile. Multiple users find solace in detailed reports and holistic views of company finances through a unified dashboard. The software is adept at generating mobile-responsive and print-friendly billing and invoice solutions, as well as trade summaries, profit and loss sheets. Harness this unique reporting feature to design personalized reports and tailored feeds, ensuring that you have your finger on the financial pulse of your business.

Tailored Permissions and Integrations

QuickBooks Online places the reins in your hands, allowing you to manage users, customize permissions, and meticulously track payments, sales history, and invoice particulars, all within an intuitive dashboard. Embrace a seamless experience as QuickBooks Online effortlessly integrates with an array of third-party applications like Intuit GoPayment,

QuickBooks Online Payroll, Shopify, Xero, Salesforce, Square POS, and more. Step into the future of financial management, where collaboration and efficiency converge seamlessly.

Unveiling QuickBooks Pricing

As of October 2022, QuickBooks Desktop undergoes a transformation in its product selection. One-time purchase licenses are retired, making way for Pro Plus and Premier Plus subscriptions, the new faces of QuickBooks Pro and Premier.

The era of one-time QuickBooks Desktop purchases is now a chapter in history. Welcome to a new age of financial software evolution.

The updated version and pricing details for QuickBooks Desktop are now available. Note that no discounts apply to any desktop goods; the full Manufacturer's Suggested Retail Price (MSRP) is standard across all distribution channels.

Simple Start	Essentials	Plus
Start your business	Run your business	Grow your business
US$18	US$27	US$38
US$9/mo*	**US$13**^{50}/mo*	**US$19**/mo*
Save US$9 for 3 months	Save US$14 for 3 months	Save US$19 for 3 months

QuickBooks Online Subscription Pricing

Embarking on your journey with QuickBooks Online is a voyage filled with choices. Whether you're initiating a brand-new small business venture or migrating your existing financial records into the digital realm, we offer a range of subscription options tailored to suit your evolving business needs.

Here, we'll navigate through the various subscription levels of QuickBooks Online, providing insight into their unique attributes and associated costs, helping you discover the ideal version of QuickBooks for your small business.

Keep in mind that pricing may vary for each product, and you can find detailed pricing information online.

1. Self-Employed: Tailored for Freelancers and Independent Contractors

QuickBooks Self-Employed caters specifically to freelancers and independent contractors who file a Schedule C form alongside their annual 1040 tax returns. This streamlined version of QuickBooks allows you to seamlessly import transactions from your bank accounts and credit cards, efficiently segregating business and personal expenses. As you categorize your business transactions, QuickBooks will also estimate your quarterly tax payments, aiding in avoiding late fees.

Moreover, this powerful tool is your ally in tracking mileage without draining your mobile device's battery.

Capture expense receipts with ease through the mobile app, utilizing QuickBooks' receipt capture tool to optimize deductions during tax time.

You can even create and send invoices to track sales, with the option to activate QuickBooks Payments, enabling credit card and bank transfer acceptance right within the invoice (additional fees apply).

It's worth noting that QuickBooks Self-Employed costs $15 per month, offering the flexibility of internet access from anywhere and customer support via live chat and email.

This subscription is a significant upgrade for those who currently rely on Excel for tracking, store receipts haphazardly, or lack an organized system for managing their business finances in preparation for Schedule-C form filing.

It's essential to acknowledge that QuickBooks Self-Employed is not suitable for businesses managing open invoices, bills across customer and vendor lists, payments to contractors or employees, inventory tracking, or the need for a custom chart of accounts with in-depth financial reporting.

If your business aligns with these requirements, consider a different subscription level.

2. Simple Start: Ideal for Small Business Owners with Basic Accounting Needs

QuickBooks Online Simple Start is designed to support a diverse range of small businesses, including sole proprietors, LLCs, and partnerships. It allows the configuration of up to 250 accounts in the chart of accounts to accommodate your unique business needs.

However, it is most suitable for solo-entrepreneur small business owners with fundamental accounting requirements. Utilize Simple Start to meticulously track income and expenses by securely importing transactions from your bank and credit card accounts. Create custom rules to automatically categorize transactions, reducing data entry and ensuring your books remain current.

This subscription empowers you to generate unlimited estimates, invoices, and sales receipts. You have the option to accept credit card and bank transfer payments using QuickBooks Payments (additional fees apply). Craft custom invoices using sales form templates and track up to three custom fields.

Simple Start facilitates the tracking of accounts receivable, offers a comprehensive sales monitoring feature, and allows you to monitor cash flow. It even calculates sales tax rates automatically, ensuring compliance and simplifying the process of filing sales tax returns. Capture, email, or photograph your receipts, and QuickBooks' receipt capture tool will assist you in categorizing expenses efficiently. Plus, you can create sales transactions on the go through the mobile app and get an at-a-glance view of your sales. While Simple Start supports one user, you can invite up to two accounting firms to review your books at no additional cost.

Additionally, you can enhance your subscription with payroll features for prompt payment to employees and 1099 contractors via 24-hour direct deposit, complete with payroll tax management right within QuickBooks (additional fees apply).

Monitor the health of your business through over 20 reports and set up automated report emailing, even to users not using QuickBooks. It's essential to note that Simple Start may not align with businesses that involve multiple users, inventory management, purchase orders, tracking billable time and expenses, accounts payable management, project tracking for job costing, budget creation, multiple currency management, or require more in-depth reporting. If your business falls into these categories, consider a different subscription level.

3. Essentials: Enhanced Functionality for Small Businesses with Diverse Needs

QuickBooks Online Essentials builds upon the features of Simple Start while introducing additional capabilities for businesses with diverse requirements. This subscription level offers support for managing multiple users, allowing you to add up to three users and configure their access.

Moreover, employees and contractors can access time tracking features, ensuring accurate time entry. These users are separate from the three-user limit and have distinct login credentials, allowing QuickBooks to maintain a comprehensive audit log. Essentials further facilitates payroll hour entry, enabling you to mark billable hours for seamless integration into invoices. You can enter vendor bills, monitor accounts payable, and execute batch payments for multiple bills simultaneously.

Access detailed reports showcasing your outstanding payables and receivables. Additionally, the option to pay vendor bills electronically is available through Bill Pay powered by Bill.com (additional fees apply). Essentials equips you with the ability to create recurring transactions, offering automation to save you time and effort.

Create invoices, sales receipts, bills, and more automatically based on a schedule, template, or reminders. International business activities are also accommodated, with multi-currency income and expense tracking, accompanied by real-time exchange rate updates.

This subscription level offers over 40 reports for tracking business health, with the option to share custom reports with other users. While Essentials comes at double the price of Simple Start, it provides multi-user capabilities, bill management, time tracking, billable time tracking, and enhanced automation features.

It's essential to recognize that Essentials may not align with businesses that require inventory management, purchase orders, billable expense tracking, project job costing, custom budget creation, multiple currency management, or seek more comprehensive reporting. If your business falls into these categories, consider a different subscription level.

4. Plus: Comprehensive Features for Growing Businesses

QuickBooks Online Plus encompasses all the attributes of Simple Start and Essentials, delivering enhanced functionality suitable for small businesses with more intricate requirements.

This subscription is the most popular among QuickBooks Online users. Plus extends support for managing multiple users, allowing you to have up to five users with customized access configurations. You can also invite users for reporting and time tracking

QuickBooks offers you a choice between two enticing options to kickstart your accounting journey. You can opt for an exclusive 50 percent discount for the initial three months of your selected subscription, which translates to substantial savings.

Alternatively, you can explore QuickBooks with a risk-free 30-day trial, during which you might even be presented with a discount offer. If your intention is to use QuickBooks consistently for your business, it's advisable to consider the discounted plan, as such offers may not be available during your trial period. On the other hand, the 30-day trial is a golden opportunity to thoroughly evaluate the software and its suitability for your needs, all without any financial commitment.

Should you find that QuickBooks doesn't align with your requirements, you can easily cancel your subscription, but please note that the trial concludes on the 30th day.

Let's Compare QuickBooks Features

QuickBooks boasts a plethora of features tailored for optimal user experience, each designed to cater to specific business needs. Here's a brief overview of these features and their implications in the sections that follow:

QuickBooks Online Self-Employed

Ideal for independent contractors like real estate agents, Uber and Lyft drivers, and freelancers, QuickBooks Self-Employed offers secure access from any internet-connected device, similar to QuickBooks Online. It stands out with unique capabilities, such as tracking both business and personal expenses from the same bank account.

Additionally, it seamlessly integrates with TurboTax, simplifying tax-related tasks. The platform even calculates expected quarterly tax payments and sends timely reminders.

QuickBooks Simple Start

QuickBooks Simple Start is a boon for business owners, providing essential bookkeeping functions like billing and expense management. Users can access reports, track income and expenses, and send invoices, all within a unified online interface. By automating these processes, the platform reduces administrative time and minimizes the risk of errors. From managing 1099 contractors to basic reporting, receipt management, and sales tracking, Simple Start covers a wide array of bookkeeping tasks.

QuickBooks Online Essentials

Tailored for businesses with up to three users, QuickBooks Online Essentials handles accounts receivable, income, spending, and payables efficiently. It facilitates accounts payable aging reports, enabling businesses to stay ahead of bill due dates. Moreover, users can seamlessly collaborate with accountants, streamlining tax-related procedures. The key distinction from QuickBooks Online Plus lies in the user limit (three users for Essentials and five for Plus) and specific features, with Plus offering inventory management and advanced project profitability tracking.

QuickBooks Online Plus

For businesses dealing in both goods and services, QuickBooks Online Plus reigns supreme.

It encompasses all the features of Simple Start and Essentials while adding advanced functionalities.

Users can monitor inventory costs and quantities, create purchase orders, and delve into detailed project profitability analysis, including labor costs, payroll, and expenses. QuickBooks Online Plus empowers seamless communication with accountants, ensuring a smooth tax season.

Each QuickBooks version caters to distinct business requirements, providing tailored solutions to enhance productivity and streamline financial operations.

Essentials, and Plus

Among the available QuickBooks plans, Essentials and Plus are the intermediate choices. The key distinction between QuickBooks Essentials and Plus lies in their target audience. Essentials caters to service-based businesses without tangible goods to sell, focusing on tracking revenue, managing bills, controlling expenses, and streamlining payment collection.

On the other hand, Plus is designed for businesses, both product-based and service-based, that require project profitability management, purchase order creation, and inventory tracking. This enhanced plan also offers more advanced reporting capabilities.

Both Essentials and Plus come with the convenience of free mobile apps, allowing you to manage your business while on the move. These subscriptions also include automated workflows, industry-specific reports, and automatic data backup for added peace of mind.

QuickBooks Online Advanced

QuickBooks Online Advanced stands as the most powerful version of QuickBooks Online, tailored to businesses with complex financial and accounting needs. It empowers you with deeper insights, enhanced peace of mind, and increased productivity, allowing you to focus on critical decision-making and elevate your business to the next level.As a cloud-based accounting software, QuickBooks Online Advanced includes all essential accounting functions found in QuickBooks. It also offers robust tools such as customizable business analytics, revenue and cash flow dashboards, bespoke user roles for up to 25 individuals, and online backup and data restoration capabilities. With features like batch invoicing and automated workflows, QuickBooks Online Advanced helps you save time and money. Furthermore, the mobile app ensures that your employees can access real-time data from multiple locations and efficiently track mileage.

QuickBooks Online Accountant

QuickBooks Online Accountant is cloud-based software designed for accounting practices, aiding bookkeepers and accountants in the editing, auditing, and correction of customer transactions. Accounting professionals can join the QuickBooks Online ProAdvisor program for free upon registration. QuickBooks Online Accountant combines comprehensive bookkeeping capabilities, offering client tools along with an advanced feature set from QuickBooks Online Advanced to meet a wide range of bookkeeping needs.

Some of the key benefits of QuickBooks Online Accountant include:

- Ideal for businesses and accountants seeking free accounting practice management software.

- Enables businesses to manage both their clients' finances and their own operations from a single dashboard.

- Provides a unique Find-a-ProAdvisor profile for professionals to promote their services, complemented by Intuit Marketing Hub resources.

With this knowledge in hand, you're well-acquainted with QuickBooks Online and its various editions. The upcoming chapters will delve deeper into the capabilities of QuickBooks Online and QuickBooks Online Accountant (QBOA), featuring practical exercises to enhance your understanding. So, take notes, read attentively, study, and practice to make the most of this resource!

QuickBooks Tutorial Tips for Beginners

Entering the world of QuickBooks can be daunting for newcomers, but remember that Rome wasn't built in a day. Learning QuickBooks is a journey best taken step by step, and online QuickBooks training can be a valuable companion along the way.

The good news is, once you've mastered the basics, QuickBooks will streamline your accounting and bookkeeping tasks, making them simpler and more transparent. To embark on this journey, consider these helpful tips:

1. Set Clear Daily Objectives

If you're venturing into QuickBooks on your own, take it one step at a time. Break your learning process into manageable pieces. For example:

- Day 1: Familiarize yourself with the software and navigate the interface. Complete the QuickBooks Getting Started Tutorial.

- Day 2: Begin entering your business information, set up accounts, and organize your data. Learn how to input customer and employee details.

- Day 3: Master tasks like invoicing, entering expenses, and payments. Explore financial statement navigation, reconciliation, check printing, and bill payments via QuickBooks.

- Day 4: Customize and automate transactions.

- Day 5: Dive into 3rd-party app integrations and explore compatible applications.

2. Utilize QuickBooks' Getting Started Tutorials

QuickBooks provides a user-friendly Getting Started Tutorial. This tutorial guides you through essential functions such as inputting data, invoicing, bill payments, and more.

These tutorials are tailored for beginners and offer an easy-to-follow introduction to the software. If you ever feel that tutorials alone don't suffice and navigating the software is daunting, online QuickBooks training becomes an invaluable resource. Professional training minimizes the learning curve, eliminates guesswork, and ensures you grasp the software inside and out.

3. Build a Foundation in Accounting Principles

Before you dive into QuickBooks, having a basic understanding of accounting principles can be highly beneficial. While you don't need to become an accounting expert (that's where your professional accountant and certified bookkeeper come in), understanding financial reporting rules and guidelines can set you up for success.

This knowledge enables you to generate accurate financial data and make informed financial decisions.

Basic accounting and bookkeeping principles ensure consistent and high-quality financial information for your business.

4. Harness QuickBooks Keyboard Shortcuts

Gone are the days of manual entry on paper. QuickBooks makes life easier, and keyboard shortcuts are one way it achieves this. Try these commonly used shortcuts (in alphabetical order):

QuickBooks Shortcuts

- Ctrl+A: Opens the Chart of Accounts window.

- Ctrl+C: Copies your selection to the Clipboard.

- Ctrl+D: Deletes checks, invoices, transactions, or items.

- Ctrl+E: Edits the selected transaction in the register.

- Ctrl+F: Opens the Find window.

- Ctrl+I: Creates an invoice.

- Ctrl+J: Opens the Customer Center.

- Ctrl+M: Memorizes transactions or reports.

- Ctrl+N: Creates new invoices, bills, checks, or list items in context.

- Ctrl+Q: Generates a QuickReport on a transaction or list item.

- Ctrl+T: Opens the memorized transaction list.

- Ctrl+W: Opens the Write Checks window.

- Ctrl+X: Moves your selection to the Clipboard.

- Ctrl+Insert: Inserts a line into a list of items or expenses.

- Ctrl+Delete: Deletes the selected line from a list of items or expenses.

5. Customize QuickBooks to Suit Your Needs

Once you're comfortable with the basics, consider customizing the software to fit your business needs. Utilize ready-made templates to personalize invoices and spreadsheets to your preferences. Customize your icon bar by adding, removing, or modifying icons to enhance your efficiency and find the links you need quickly. Creating a customized icon bar tailored to your most frequently used features can save you time and streamline your operations.

Here's a brief guide on customizing your icon bar:

To remove an icon:

- Select 'View' and click 'Customize Icon Bar.'

- Choose the icon you wish to remove and click 'Delete.'

To add an icon:

- Select 'View' and click 'Customize Icon Bar.'

- Click 'Add' and select your desired icon from the list.

- Modify the label and description, then click 'OK.'

To modify an icon:

- Select 'View' and click 'Customize Icon Bar.'

- Choose the icon you wish to modify.

- Click 'Edit,' make your changes, and click 'OK.'

6. Consistently Reconcile QuickBooks Accounts

Regular reconciliation is one of the most crucial aspects of using QuickBooks. This practice ensures that all transactions and bank account details are accurately recorded, guaranteeing that your financial statements maintain their accuracy. Allocate time for periodic reviews—weekly, quarterly, and annually—to stay in control of your finances and track your expenditures efficiently.

7. Back Up Your Work

Don't overlook this essential step—backing up your data. It's a safeguard against unexpected data loss. QuickBooks offers automatic scheduled backups to ensure your work is always saved. If you use QuickBooks Online, the cloud-based program allows you to access your files from anywhere with an internet connection. Cloud accounting not only provides mobility but also ensures your data remains secure. While data on a local computer can be lost in case of a crash, cloud accounting ensures that your records are automatically and safely stored in the cloud.

8. Learn QuickBooks from Various Sources

Lastly, consider learning QuickBooks through multiple avenues. Diverse learning methods can deepen your understanding and mastery of the software.

Quickbooks and How It Benefits Small Businesses

QuickBooks has proven to be the software of choice for small businesses due to its ease of use. In comparison to other modern and complex accounting systems, it is also a cost-effective accounting system.

Many company owners have found it to be a useful tool in managing their money.

It is capable of handling all areas of accounting. Payroll, fixed asset management, inventory management, and other services are among them.

This QuickBooks training is a wonderful way to get started with accounting for small businesses. It will keep track of your income and spending as well as day-to-day transactions. It's so simple to understand that you can pick up the fundamentals and start using them the next day.

Key Benefits to Small Businesses

QuickBooks will automatically record your income and keep track of how much each customer owes you. You can see how many outstanding bills you have, often known as your accounts receivable. Invoices are simple to make and can be printed or sent to customers.

QuickBooks automatically keeps track of your bills and spending by linking your bank and credit card accounts to QuickBooks, which downloads and categorizes all of your expenses.

If you need to manually monitor a check or cash transaction, you may do so in a matter of minutes in QuickBooks.

You may produce financial statements that give important information about how your firm is operating if you manage all of your cash input and outflow operations in QuickBooks.

You will understand how to create a profit and loss report. It will show you how profitable your company is by aggregating its income and subtracting its costs. The report displays the bottom line net income for a specified period, such as a week, a month, or a quarter.

Employees or subcontractors can input their own time as they work throughout the day, or if the employee submits a manual timesheet, a bookkeeper can enter their weekly time.

The time that has been entered and allocated to a customer will be available for inclusion in the client's next invoice.

Any expenditure can be designated as chargeable and assigned to a client. These billable items, like time, will be available to add to the next invoice for the client. To track employee hours for invoicing purposes, the payroll add-on isn't required.

The QuickBooks online training will help you keep track of your inventory's quantity and cost using the software. When inventory levels are low, QuickBooks may automatically remind you to buy more.

The most essential thing QuickBooks training can accomplish for your small business is to make tax time less complicated. Compiling your income and spending is by far the most difficult part of completing a tax return.

If you use QuickBooks throughout the year, you just have to print your financial statements around tax time. You may give your tax accountant immediate access to your account using QuickBooks Online, allowing them to evaluate your figures and print any information they need to complete your return.

The QuickBooks online training will is also offering consumers the opportunity to pay their bills online is one of the finest methods to boost your cash flow.

Customers may pay online immediately from their emailed invoice by using QuickBooks Payments. Other merchant services are comparable to QuickBooks Payments. Because it's fully integrated with QuickBooks, the sales, credit card fees, and cash deposits are all instantly recorded as they happen.

Being able to arrange your receipts in QuickBooks is another essential to having tax season go smoothly. All QuickBooks online users may get the QuickBooks app for free, take a photo of a receipt, and upload it in a matter of minutes.

You may connect a receipt to the related banking transaction in QuickBooks. Because the receipts are saved in the cloud with your data, you may upload an infinite number of receipts to QuickBooks Online.

CHAPTER 2

See How Small Businesses Use QuickBooks

1. Create, Send & Monitor Invoices

With QuickBooks Online, all plans enable you to effortlessly generate and distribute invoices to your customers. You can either print these invoices or send them via email. QuickBooks automatically records your income and keeps track of each customer's outstanding balances. You can also check the status of your accounts receivable (A/R) and identify overdue invoices by running an A/R aging report.

You can create invoices from scratch or convert existing estimates into invoices. Furthermore, you have the flexibility to customize your invoices by altering colors and adding your company's logo.

2. Keep Tabs on Bills & Expenses

QuickBooks simplifies the tracking of your bills and expenses. By linking your bank and credit card accounts to QuickBooks, your expenses are automatically downloaded and categorized. In case you need to record a check or cash transaction manually, QuickBooks provides a straightforward process.

For incoming bills, you can enter them into QuickBooks as you receive them, ensuring efficient tracking of upcoming payments. QuickBooks enables you to stay on top of your bill payments by generating accounts payable (A/P) reports that detail both current and overdue bills. The ability to pay bills and track outstanding expenses is available in QuickBooks Essentials and higher subscription plans.

3. Online Bill Payments

QuickBooks offers an online bill payment feature, available in QuickBooks Online Essentials and above. With QuickBooks Online Bill Pay, you can swiftly pay bills through bank transfers or checks directly from the QuickBooks platform, streamlining the payment process. You can also make payments to vendors and suppliers using a credit card. QuickBooks Online Bill Pay is fully integrated with QuickBooks Essentials, Plus, and Advanced.

To initiate your first online bill payment, you'll need to input your bank account information, select your preferred payment method, and specify your vendor's payment preferences. QuickBooks Online will then automatically use this information for future transactions, reducing manual data entry. Paid bills will be marked as such in QuickBooks, keeping your outstanding bills list up to date.

To pay bills online, start by entering your bills in QuickBooks Online and then use the "+ New" button to select "Pay bills online."

4. Customize Expense Categories With a Chart of Accounts

QuickBooks employs a chart of accounts to manage all your accounts for tracking financial data. This includes accounts for income, expenses, assets, liabilities, and equity, all of which may be necessary for your tax return.

An appropriately structured Chart of Accounts can facilitate your tax preparation. In addition to standard line items, you can customize your Chart of Accounts to provide valuable insights that support your business management. You can find guidance on adding, removing, and customizing accounts in the "How To Set Up a Chart of Accounts in QuickBooks Online" tutorial.

5. Print Financial Statements for Your Business

QuickBooks helps you produce financial statements that offer valuable insights into your business's performance by tracking all cash inflows and outflows. Financial statements are often required by lenders when applying for small business loans or lines of credit.

QuickBooks allows you to generate three primary financial statements:

- Profit and Loss Report: This report summarizes your income minus expenses, providing a snapshot of your net income (or loss) for a specific period.

- Balance Sheet Report: This report provides a snapshot of your business's financial position, including assets, liabilities, and equity.

- Statement of Cash Flows: This report details the movement of cash in and out of your business during a specific period.

You can refer to the snapshots of these reports provided within QuickBooks Online for a more comprehensive view.

6. Track Employee Time & Expenses

QuickBooks makes it easy to track employee time and expenses. Employees or subcontractors can enter their own time as they work, or you can record their hours manually if they submit a timesheet. Time entries assigned to a customer can be included in that customer's next invoice.

Additionally, expenses can be marked as billable and associated with a specific customer. These billable expenses can be seamlessly added to your next invoice for that customer. QuickBooks provides this functionality starting with QuickBooks Essentials for billable hours and QuickBooks Plus for billable expenses.

7. Project Profitability Monitoring

With QuickBooks Online Plus or Advanced, you can create and manage projects, allocate income and wages to projects, and track expenses related to labor and materials.

The project accounting module in QuickBooks Online allows you to create project estimates, incorporating inventory, labor, and sales taxes.

While you can't compare actual and estimated costs directly in QuickBooks Online, you can monitor the profitability of each project you're working on by generating a project profitability summary report.

8. Payroll Management

Running payroll manually can lead to costly errors and dissatisfied employees. QuickBooks offers an integrated payroll function that automates payroll calculations and processing, ensuring accuracy and timeliness.

As you enter employee time, whether for billable hours or expenses, QuickBooks automatically updates the payroll module. Payroll data is integrated into your financial statements, keeping them up to date. To access the payroll features, you'll need to subscribe to a QuickBooks Payroll service, which offers various service levels to meet your needs.

QuickBooks Payroll allows you to:

- Pay employees via check or direct deposit

- Automatically calculate federal and state payroll taxes

- Generate payroll tax forms

- E-pay your payroll taxes directly through QuickBooks

9. Inventory Tracking

QuickBooks offers inventory management features in the Plus and Advanced subscription plans. This functionality helps you monitor inventory quantity and costs accurately.

As you sell inventory, QuickBooks automatically allocates a portion of your inventory to the cost of goods sold (COGS), an expense account that reduces your income.

This allocation is essential for calculating taxable income and can be challenging to perform manually.

QuickBooks can also assist you in managing inventory by providing automatic reminders to reorder items when stock levels are low.

10. Simplify Tax Preparation

One of the most significant advantages of using QuickBooks for your small business is simplifying tax preparation. By keeping your financial records up to date throughout the year, tax time becomes a breeze.

QuickBooks helps you efficiently organize your income and expenses, making it easier to complete your tax return.

With QuickBooks Online, you can also grant your tax preparer direct access to your account, allowing them to review your financial data and access the necessary information to prepare your tax return.

11. Accept Online Payments

Enhance your cash flow by offering your customers the convenience of paying their invoices online. QuickBooks allows you to integrate QuickBooks Payments (formerly Intuit Merchant Services), enabling customers to make online payments directly from emailed invoices.

QuickBooks Payments streamlines the entire process, as it's fully integrated with QuickBooks. Every sale, credit card fee, and deposit are automatically recorded, ensuring that your records are always up to date.

12. Receipt Scanning

Simplify tax time further by easily organizing your receipts in QuickBooks. All QuickBooks Online subscribers can utilize the free QuickBooks mobile app to capture receipts using their mobile devices. You can then upload these receipts to QuickBooks Online quickly.

QuickBooks enables you to link receipts to corresponding banking transactions and provides cloud storage for unlimited receipt uploads.

13. Mileage Tracking

Tracking business mileage is essential for tax deductions. QuickBooks Online offers a straightforward solution. The QuickBooks mobile app uses your phone's GPS to automatically detect when you're in a moving vehicle, making mileage tracking effortless.

You can review your trips and classify them as personal or business. For billable trips, QuickBooks will automatically add mileage expenses to your next customer invoice.

14. App Integration

QuickBooks Online seamlessly integrates with a wide range of business applications available in the QuickBooks App Store. These integrations can help simplify various aspects of your business, from managing bills and accepting payments to forecasting cash flow.

In addition to native QuickBooks Online integrations like QuickBooks Payroll, QuickBooks Time, and QuickBooks Payments, QuickBooks Online connects with popular third-party apps. Some of these integrations include PayPal, Melio, HubSpot, Expensify, LeanLaw, Square Payroll, and Expensify.

15. Mobile Accounting

The QuickBooks Online mobile app allows you to perform accounting tasks on the go. Available for Android and iOS devices, the app empowers you to create and send invoices, accept online payments, and allocate expenses to projects or customers.

You can also track your business mileage and access financial reports directly from your smartphone. Please note that an active QuickBooks Online subscription is required to utilize these features.

16. Collaborate With a QuickBooks ProAdvisor

Collaborating with a QuickBooks ProAdvisor can enhance the efficiency and accuracy of your accounting and financial management processes. QuickBooks ProAdvisors are certified professionals with extensive knowledge of the software's features and capabilities.

They can assist with setting up your accounting procedures, troubleshooting issues, and maximizing QuickBooks' functionality. QuickBooks users can invite accountants to access their books, and QuickBooks Desktop users can export and import changes made by accountants.

To find a QuickBooks ProAdvisor, you can search on Intuit's "Find a ProAdvisor" website, which provides step-by-step guidance. You can also explore other platforms to discover ProAdvisors.

Alternatively, you can engage a QuickBooks ProAdvisor through QuickBooks Live, an add-on to QuickBooks Online. QuickBooks Live offers flexible pricing based on your company's monthly expenses and allows you to customize services with an independent ProAdvisor.

17. Sales Tax Management

QuickBooks assists small businesses in managing their sales tax responsibilities. It calculates sales tax, prepares sales tax returns, and generates sales tax liability reports. The system can automatically calculate sales tax for transactions based on customer locations and applicable tax rates and rules.

QuickBooks can also integrate with popular sales tax software providers, such as Avalara and TaxJar, to streamline sales tax management and ensure compliance with local and state tax regulations. This capability is valuable for businesses selling products or services in multiple jurisdictions, as it can calculate and track sales tax rates and rules for each jurisdiction

Setting Up Your QuickBooks Online Company

When you first log in to QuickBooks Online, you'll be guided through the process of creating your company. You can start by entering your information from scratch, importing data from

QuickBooks Desktop if needed, or importing lists like customers, vendors, and inventory items.

Getting Started with QuickBooks Online

Now that you've decided to use QuickBooks for your company, it's essential to ensure that your QuickBooks Online activities align with your real-world business operations. This includes all transactions, from tracking sales to making bank deposits. While some tasks, such as invoicing, are done entirely within QuickBooks, most transactions reflect activities that have occurred elsewhere.

It's crucial to maintain accurate accounting records for each stage of a transaction, whether you're processing credit card payments, managing payroll with QuickBooks Payroll, or securing a loan from a bank. This involves reconciling recorded transactions with your actual bank statements, cross-referencing names, dates, payment methods, and totals.

Here's how to get started:

1. Visit quickbooks.intuit.com/pricing.

2. Look for the four subscription options: Simple Start, Essentials, Plus, and Advanced. If you're interested in QuickBooks Self-Employed, scroll down to the freelancer and independent contractor section. You can choose between a 30-day free trial or a three-month reduced price plan for Simple Start, Essentials, and Plus.

Note that the Advanced subscription doesn't offer a free trial, but you can access it at qbo.intuit.com/redir/testdrive_us_advanced.

By selecting the free trial option, you can try QuickBooks for 30 days at no cost. Keep in mind that choosing to purchase the software immediately may provide more significant savings compared to using free trials, as discounts typically apply to paid subscriptions. Also, be aware that promotional pricing often ends after three months.

Exploring Your New Company

In QuickBooks Online, companies function much like those in the physical business world. Here are some essential characteristics:

- Access your company's dashboard by logging into your QuickBooks account.

- Click the gear icon to find "Account and Settings."

- Select the "Company" tab within the "Account and Settings" section.

Company Name:

- To modify your company name, click anywhere within the company name area, including the pencil icon.

- Save your changes after making the necessary adjustments.

In the company name section, you'll find three items:

Company Logo:

- You can import your company's logo to include it on the forms you create. To do this, follow these steps:

- Click the gray square next to the company logo.

- The logos you've previously uploaded to QuickBooks Online will be displayed on the next screen. If your desired logo isn't shown, click the blue plus sign to include it.

- QuickBooks will guide you through selecting the logo image file from your computer.

- After selecting the image file, you'll see a thumbnail of your new logo. The logo is then saved in your QuickBooks Online account, eliminating the need to refresh it when customizing forms.

- Ensure that your chosen logo is highlighted, then click the "Save" button.

Company and Legal Name:

- Enter your company name as you wish it to appear on forms and invoices. This should match the name you've registered with the IRS for your business. The legal name is used on tax documents like Form 1099 and payroll tax returns.

If your legal name differs from the name you want to appear on invoices, uncheck the box and enter your legal name.

EIN (Employer Identification Number):

- Ensure that the IRS number matches your official records. If you're self-employed, use your Social Security number. Due to the sensitivity of EINs, QuickBooks may require additional authentication before accessing or editing this number.

Company Type:

- To input or modify your company type, click the pencil icon or any other area in the Company Type section.

- Select your taxable entity type from the drop-down menu adjacent to the "Tax form" field. You can choose from the following options based on your business structure:

  - Sole Proprietorship

  - Partnership

  - S Corporation (S-Corp)

  - C Corporation (C-Corp)

  - Nonprofit Organization

  - Limited Liability Company (LLC)

Company's Contact Information:

- To enter contact information for QuickBooks and your clients, click anywhere in the "Contact info" section, including the pencil icon.

Email: QuickBooks uses your business email to contact the administrator. The customer-facing email address, which appears on your clients' sales forms like invoices, can be different from the QuickBooks administrator's email. If needed, uncheck the option and enter the correct address.

Company Phone: Enter the phone number to be printed on sales forms provided to customers.

Website: Enter your website address to appear on all sales forms.

Company Address: To input or modify your company's address information, click the pencil icon or any other location in the address area. In QuickBooks Online, the corporate address, customer-facing address, and legal address are listed separately.

- Company Address: This is the physical address of the business, used for sending payments to QuickBooks.

- Customer-Facing Address: This address is visible on invoices and sales documents, and it's where clients should send their payments.

If it differs from your corporate address, uncheck the box and provide the correct customer-facing address.

- Legal Address: Your tax filings must use the legal address that matches the one on record with the IRS. If different from the company address, uncheck the option and provide the legal address. Click the green Save button to save changes.

Reviewing the QuickBooks Interface: If you're transitioning from QuickBooks Desktop to QuickBooks Online, you may notice differences in the user interface. Despite these visual disparities, both systems have identical functionality.

QuickBooks Online's streamlined design simplifies accounting once you become familiar with it. The key components are the header bar and navigation bar.

Header Bar: The header bar appears at the top, offering navigation options. The "+" icon allows you to enter new transactions, categorized under Customers, Vendors, Employees, and Others. The "gear icon" provides access to budgeting, audit logs, settings, limits, and import/export options.

Navigation Bar: The vertical navigation bar on the left provides quick access to features like Banking, Sales, Expenses, Workers, and Reports.

In QuickBooks Online, you enter transactions individually via the "+ icon," unlike QuickBooks Desktop, which allows direct input into a bank register.

Updating the Chart of Accounts: The chart of accounts is a list of accounts used to classify transactions. To access and review your chart of accounts, select Settings > Chart of accounts. Account types and detail types determine the data displayed on financial reports. You can also view account histories and run reports. Editing or Inactivating Accounts: Keep your chart of accounts organized. To make an account inactive, follow these steps:

1. Deactivate accounts with a zero balance or never used.

2. Correct the balance to zero for active accounts on the balance sheet.

3. If an account has subaccounts, move the subaccounts to a separate account.

Inactive accounts remain in your records but don't affect transactions. You can choose to hide inactive accounts in some reports, but this may affect accuracy.

Adding Account Numbers: You can keep your accounts organized by assigning account numbers. To enable account numbers, follow these steps:

1. Go to Settings and choose Account and settings.

2. Choose the Advanced tab option.

23 Click on Edit in the Chart of accounts section.

4. Turn on "Enable account numbers." If you want to display account numbers on reports and transactions, choose "Show account numbers."

5. Click Save and then Done.

Now that account numbers are enabled, follow these steps to use them:

1. Go to Bookkeeping and click on Chart of accounts.

2. Click on Batch edit at the top of the Action column.

3. Add account numbers in the Number column.

4. After completing the steps above, click the Save button.

With account numbers enabled, finding specific accounts in the Chart of Accounts or adding transactions will be quicker. You can use the assigned numbers to locate accounts easily.

Importing a chart of accounts:

Your chart of accounts is essential for organizing your accounting. Instead of manually entering accounts, you can import them from another QuickBooks Online or Desktop company file or a spreadsheet of custom accounts. Here's how to do it:

Formatting the spreadsheet:

1. Open an existing account spreadsheet or create a new one.

2. Make sure your spreadsheet contains columns for Account name, Type, Detail Type, and Number.

3. Add an Account Number column if you organize your accounts by numbers.

4. Save your spreadsheet in Google Sheets, Excel, or CSV format.

Uploading the spreadsheet:

1. Sign in to QuickBooks Online.

2. Go to Settings and click on Import Data.

3. Select Chart of Accounts.

4. Upload your file from your computer or from Google Sheets.

Mapping spreadsheet fields to QuickBooks fields:

After uploading your spreadsheet, you need to map your accounts to ensure they import correctly.

Here's how:

1. In the "Your Field" column, match the names to the QuickBooks Online fields for Detail Type, Account name, Account number, and Type.

2. If a field doesn't match a column in your spreadsheet, choose "No Match" (except for Account Name if you don't use account numbers).

3. Click Next.

Import your chart of accounts:

Review the settings and ensure everything is correct. If any field is highlighted in red, hover your cursor over it to see what needs to be fixed.

Uncheck any accounts you don't want to save, and then select "Import" when everything looks good.

Reviewing Company Settings:

Within your company settings, you have the ability to view and make changes to essential information such as your firm's name, address, contact details, and Employer Identification Number (EIN) on the Company tab.

Moreover, you can adjust settings related to Intuit marketing.

Company Preferences

Under Company Preferences, you can set certain parameters that impact the way QuickBooks functions. This includes usage statistics, which are limitations on the number of accounts, users, classes, locations, and tags that can be concurrently utilized based on your subscription.

These restrictions vary according to your QuickBooks Online subscription, with caps applying exclusively to active users, accounts, classes, locations, and tags.

The Usage tab provides a detailed overview of these limits. If you're an accountant, you can directly access your clients' usage limits.

To explore your usage restrictions:

1. Sign in to QuickBooks Online as an administrator.

2. Access Settings and choose Account and Settings.

3. Navigate to the Usage tab.

4. If you reach your usage caps and are unable to add more users or accounts, you have two options: upgrade your subscription level or reduce your usage. Remember to assess usage for each of your companies if you manage multiple entities.

Sales Preferences

Within the Sales tab, you have the ability to set up payment terms, customize the appearance of your sales forms, and control the information displayed on customer forms. You can also enable features like automatic reminders and progress billing.

Customizing Sales Forms

QuickBooks Online empowers you to create polished and professional invoices, estimates, and sales receipts without the need for design expertise. You can tailor the look and feel of these forms and choose the information visible to your customers. Follow these steps to create a new template:

1. Go to Settings and select Custom Form Styles.

2. Create a New style.

3. Choose the type of sales form for which you want to create a template.

Customize the appearance of your form by:

1. Accessing the Design tab.

2. Naming your template.

3. Selecting a predefined layout.

4. Making logo adjustments, including altering its size and placement.

5. Exploring different color options.

6. Changing font size.

7. Adjusting margins for printed forms.

Customizing Form Content:

Under the Content tab, you can modify different sections of the form, such as the header, table, or footer, independently.

Additionally, you c display specific fields on your form as needed.

Expenses Preferences

You can enable billable expenses and purchase orders, as well as personalize email notifications related to purchase orders, in the Expenses section.

Payment Preferences

Under the Payments tab, you can link your QuickBooks Payments account and set up online payment options.

This allows you to control merchant information and determine where QuickBooks should automatically record deposits.

Time Preferences

The Time tab lets you configure various aspects, including defining the start of the workweek, tracking services provided by your team, and deciding whether to disclose your service rates to staff and vendors.

Advanced Preferences

In the Advanced tab, you can activate additional features in QuickBooks, such as specialized tracking categories for goods and services. You can also specify your company's fiscal year start and end. Additionally, if your business deals with multiple currencies, this is where you enable this functionality.

QuickBooks Online Apps

Under the Apps tab, you can conveniently select and switch applications for your business and clients from a single location.

Discovering Apps

1. From the menu's left side, select "Apps."

2. Navigate to the "Find Apps" tab.

3. To locate specific apps, either type their names into the search field or choose a category from the browse drop-down menu.

Installing an App

1. Once you've found your preferred app, click on its title to view reviews and pricing.

2. To initiate the signup process, click "Get App Now."

3. Choose your firm, or alternatively, select a client from the "Install for Your Client" drop-down menu.

4. Click on the "Install" button.

5. Authorize QuickBooks to share your data with the chosen app.

6. Configure any sync preferences.

7. Choose "Save & Sync."

Please note that not all applications can be synced for clients. If the selected app falls into this category, you will be alerted to this limitation. You can choose to receive notifications when the app is ready for installation for your client.

Client Apps

To examine and interact with apps currently connected to your clients' businesses, go to the "Client Apps" tab. If the app is one of the cost-effective options in the Apps Program, you might be able to activate it. To make the most of the software, activate it upon purchase.

Click on the app tile to see details about its connection and support contact information. You can take various actions from the drop-down menu:

1. Open the app.

2. Access support for the app.

3. Disconnect the app from the company.

4. Leave a review for the app. Please note that the drop-down menu is only available for connected apps.

Firm Apps

You can view or interact with apps related to your firm in the "Firm Apps" tab. You can select from the drop-down menu for actions:

1. Open the app.

2. Access support for the app.

3. Disconnect the app from the company.

4. Leave a review for the app.

QuickBooks Online Desktop App

For Microsoft Windows (64-bit required), the QuickBooks Online Advanced Desktop client offers enhanced navigation and workflow acceleration. This program provides greater stability for power users who spend extensive time using QuickBooks Online, thanks to its multi-tab and company-switching features. It is particularly valuable for QuickBooks customers who use multiple QBO accounts or access QuickBooks frequently.

If you choose to access QuickBooks Advanced through the QBO Advanced Desktop program for MSW instead of a web browser, you can remain logged in for up to six months unless you deliberately log out. After signing in, you can stay signed in, allowing you to access QBO whenever needed without repeated sign-ins.

Users will have access to a navigation map view similar to the home page workflows found in QuickBooks Desktop, providing a roadmap of connected actions and processes that can streamline workflows for some users.

Accessing numerous QuickBooks Online firms simultaneously and seamlessly switching between them without refreshing each company is another significant advantage of the new software. You can effortlessly manage all your clients, regardless of their QBO version, with this functionality.

Installation Steps:

1. Visit QBO-Accountant or QBO-Advanced and select the gear symbol to download the app. A button for downloading the desktop app will be visible.

2. Your settings may allow the app to install itself automatically. Alternatively, you might be asked to save the .exe file. In this case, select "Save" and decide where to save the file. You can then initiate the installation by opening the QuickBooks Advanced Setup file.

3. After installation, a desktop shortcut for the software is created. The application should launch immediately upon installation. If not, open the app from the shortcut.

4. Enter your user ID and password on the sign-in screen and select "Sign In."

Afterward, proceed with the following steps:

1. If you have more than one QuickBooks Online Advanced company displayed, select the firm you want to open. An error warning will appear if your user ID does not belong to a QuickBooks Online firm.

2. When using the Advanced Desktop app for the first time, you have the option to customize how QuickBooks will be displayed on the home page. (You can change this setting later at any time.)

It's important to note that QuickBooks Desktop-like navigational tools are available for examining accounts. The map view offers swift navigation to essential work areas by displaying QuickBooks Online operations such as sales, costs, payroll, and reporting in workflow diagrams.

3. Within the app, you can choose either "Map View" or "Dashboard View" to switch between the navigation map view and the QuickBooks Online dashboard view.

QuickBooks Online Mobile Apps

In this era of working from home, many people find it challenging to escape the "office." However, there are times when having access to your QuickBooks Online accounting information can be incredibly useful, even when you're not at home or at your regular workplace.

This is where free companion apps for the QuickBooks Online website come into play. The QuickBooks Online mobile app is available for both iOS and Android and provides many of the same features as the desktop or laptop version. Actions you take on the app are automatically synchronized with the browser-based version, and vice versa.

Both versions offer a user-friendly experience, making it easy to manage tasks on your mobile device with a consistent design and functionality.

Upon downloading the QuickBooks Online mobile app and entering your login information from the browser-based version, you'll find a screen full of shortcuts to the program's primary features.

While this is a concise overview of everything you can accomplish, it directs you to the screens you'll use most frequently.

If you select the "All" tab, you'll find a complete list of links for the program, including features like "Reports" and "Products & Services" that are not on the shortcuts page.

The app opens two more panels when you:

- Click the home icon in the lower left corner.

- One of these panels is a dashboard that resembles the one you see in your browser. It displays your account balances and charts for profit and loss, invoices, and costs. For a list of the most recent activities, select the "Activity" tab. This list is interactive, just like most features of the app. Clicking on an activity opens the corresponding transaction.

- At the bottom of the screen, you'll find two more navigation links:

- Click the plus (+) symbol to add a transaction.

- Click the three horizontal lines to access the "Shortcuts" page.

You can also access the "Settings" screen by clicking the gear icon in the top left corner, where you'll find links to sections like "Company Information," "Tax Rates," "Overdue Invoice Alerts," and others.

QuickBooks App Store

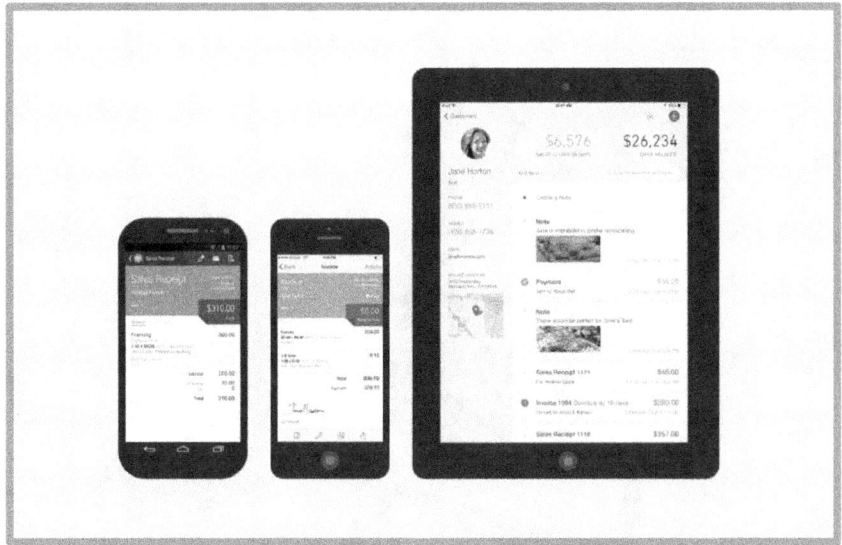

QuickBooks Essentials includes access to the QuickBooks App Store. To access it, follow the steps below that match your web browser:

- Google Chrome: Press Ctrl + Shift + N

- Mozilla Firefox: Press Ctrl + Shift + P

- Internet Explorer: Press Ctrl + Shift + P

- Safari: Press Command + Shift + N

For enhanced efficiency, clear your default browser's cache if you can see the Apps menu.

However, the site will not appear in the list if you are referring to the App Store. In that case, you will need to visit their website directly to access it.

QuickBooks Labs

As part of the QuickBooks Online update, Intuit introduced QuickBooks Labs. This feature is categorized as an experimental plug-in and involves QuickBooks integration. To safeguard your QuickBooks data, it's advisable to run the plug-in with a test company file initially.

Please be aware that QuickBooks Online does not provide an easy way to create a backup copy of your data, so you would need to rely on Intuit to protect your data.

If the plug-in causes issues, you won't be able to restore your data independently. Furthermore, there is no option in QuickBooks Online to restrict QuickBooks users from enabling such a plug-in. The platform does not offer settings to restrict access to this or similar services for users with "normal" access. One drawback is that experiments may occasionally disappear from the application, which can be disruptive if you grow accustomed to using a feature that later ceases to work.

Users may be directed to a brief instructional video before using one of the new experimental plug-ins. After selecting the "Learn More" option, users are taken to the "Intuit Labs" page, where the videos are created by actual Intuit employees rather than independent software developers.

Don't feel overwhelmed; we're just getting started. The journey should already be exciting. It's important to remember that QuickBooks Online allows you to simulate running a business if you don't have one already, and if you do, this program can be your all-in-one solution.

You should have already learned how to sign up for QuickBooks Online, explore the QBO user interface, create an account, and link account numbers.

Additionally, you should have learned how to set up a company and include all necessary features.

The other sections, such as QuickBooks Desktop, QuickBooks Lab, and QuickBooks Online App, should have been introduced to you. Be sure to put your knowledge into practice, as the main goal is not only to learn but to perform the tasks effectively. Join the activities and apply your knowledge.

CHAPTER 3

10 Reasons to Love Quickbooks

QuickBooks is widely recognized as powerful and invaluable software for various businesses. Over its more than two-decade existence, it has consistently saved both time and money, establishing itself as an essential tool for companies of all types and sizes.

Whether you're launching a new business or managing an existing one, QuickBooks is a must-have software that simplifies and streamlines accounting, tracking, and reporting, making the management of your company's finances significantly easier.

Here are the top 10 major advantages of QuickBooks for your business:

1. User-Friendly Design: QuickBooks boasts user-friendly software designed with customers in mind. Even if your company lacks a sizable accounting department, this software is intended to be utilized by multiple users, and its intuitive design ensures easy comprehension.

2. Effortless Tax Management: QuickBooks simplifies tax management, making the process of filing tax reports and monitoring income exceptionally straightforward.

You can trust that your tax reports will be accurate and submitted on time when using this software.

3. Continuous Enhancement: QuickBooks is continually evolving and improving. Regular updates introduce numerous enhancements that cater to various financial needs within your business.

4. Safety and Technological Adaptation: QuickBooks excels in terms of safety and adaptability to new technologies. Its transition toward becoming the finest financial software available is steady, and it can be accessed from various modern devices, providing business owners with convenience.

5. Integrated Efficiency Tools: QuickBooks offers numerous integrated tools that enhance efficiency.

These tools include helpful shortcuts and features that simplify accounting tasks, saving time and boosting productivity.

6. Promotes Innovation and Open-Mindedness: QuickBooks encourages companies to focus on product innovation and open thinking. By using this software, your company's productivity will increase, motivating employees to embrace innovation and work toward improving the company.

7. Cost-Effective: QuickBooks offers excellent value for money. While there is a multitude of software options on the market, QuickBooks stands out by saving you both effort and money, which can be redirected toward the company's benefit.

8. Continuous Expansion: QuickBooks is rapidly expanding and aims to surpass ten million active customers by the end of the decade. It prioritizes customer feedback, attracting new users through regular updates and improvements. Once you start using this software, you may never look back.

9. Automated Backup Service: QuickBooks provides a reliable automated backup service that ensures the safety and security of your financial data. You won't risk losing any critical information when using this software.

10. Small Business Focus: QuickBooks is tailored to small businesses, enabling them to grow and achieve significant profits.

It caters to the unique needs of small companies, facilitating their financial management.

How to Managing Customers, Vendors, and Employee Lists

In QuickBooks Online, as in the QuickBooks Desktop product, lists play a crucial role in storing essential background data that you'll use frequently. These lists encompass a wide range of information, including your customers, vendors, employees, products, services, accounts, and payment methods.

Let's explore how to manage these lists effectively to facilitate your day-to-day business operations.

Adding New Records to a List

To interact with your customers, suppliers, staff members, and subcontractors, QuickBooks Online provides convenient links in the Navigation bar. You can access these links by selecting "Sales" for customers, "Expenses" for vendors, and "Workers" for employees and contractors. Let's delve into the process of adding new records for customers, vendors, employees, or contractors

Creating a New Record

Customers are the lifeblood of any business, and establishing accurate customer records is vital.

QuickBooks Online also allows you to create sub-customers and assign customer types for better organization.

However, it's worth noting that vendors, employees, and other entities do not have these specific functionalities.

Follow the steps below to create a new customer record in QuickBooks Online:

Before you start creating records, ensure that the Multicurrency option is enabled if your business requires it.

Enabling this option is essential for defining the currency associated with each customer accurately. This step is crucial if you deal with multiple currencies.

These customer records serve as the foundation for your financial transactions and customer interactions. By maintaining organized and detailed customer records, you'll streamline your operations and enhance the efficiency of your business.

Here are the steps for creating a new customer record in QuickBooks Online:

1. Click on "Sales" in the Navigation bar to access the Customers page.

2. Locate and select the "New Customer" button positioned at the upper right corner of the page.

3. Fill in the required information as prompted.

4. Conclude by clicking the "Save" button to save the new customer record.

After adding the customer, you may not immediately see any transactions. QuickBooks Online (QBO) saves the customer and presents their page with transaction-related information.

To view or modify the details you just entered for the customer, you can select the "Customer Details" option.

If you wish to review the entire list of customers, click on "Sales" in the Navigation bar and then select "Customers."

You have the flexibility to mark any customer, vendor, or contractor as inactive as long as they have a zero balance. To do this, click the downward-pointing arrow labeled "Action" next to the respective entry in the list and choose "Make Inactive" from the displayed options.

You can also utilize customer types to categorize clients, even if they are not directly related. For example, if you offer special discounts to specific customers during certain times of the year, you can use customer types to streamline the process of identifying eligible customers for these discounts.

How to Use Customer Types

Utilizing customer types allows you to categorize diverse clients into specific customer groups. For example, if you offer exclusive discounts to certain customers during particular times of the year, employing customer types can simplify the process of identifying eligible recipients for these discounts.

• To create new customer types, click on the "Customer Types" button located in the upper right corner of the Customers page.

• Provide a name for your customer type and click "Save." Repeat these steps for each new customer type you wish to establish.

• To assign a customer category to a specific customer, go to the Customers page, select the customer's name, and then click on the "Details" tab.

You have the flexibility to assign the same customer type to a group of customers, eliminating the need to allocate customer types individually for each client, which can save you valuable time. Utilize the Sales by Customer Type Detail report, Sales by Customer Detail report grouped by customer type, and configure the Customer Contact List to include a column for customer types, enabling you to easily categorize and manage your customers based on their customer types.

Managing Records

This section highlights the various types of records you can work with in QuickBooks Online and provides instructions on how to effectively use them.

Browsing Lists

The functionality of the customer, vendor, and employee pages can be customized to suit your needs. The contractor page offers a more streamlined set of features and is primarily designed for searching for contractors and generating 1099s. You can efficiently sort the list of individuals, export the list to Excel, and perform various actions on specific subsets of individuals from the customer, vendor, or employee pages, which encompass all the individuals within these categories.

Creating Printable Reports

On any list page, you can effortlessly generate a straightforward report by clicking the "Print" button located just above the "Action" column.

Managing Attachments

To keep track of essential financial documents, you have the option to attach files such as contracts, 1099 forms, or receipts to customer, vendor, and employee records. You can add both text documents and images as attachments.

Simply drag and drop the desired item into the "Attachments" box located at the lower left corner of the relevant record's details page.

Alternatively, you can click the box to open the standard Windows Open dialog, allowing you to navigate to and select the attachment you wish to add. Each attachment is limited to a size of 25MB.

If you want to review previously attached documents, click the "Show Existing" link below the "Attachments" box, and QuickBooks Online will display them in a pane on the right side of the page.

Working with Multiple Records

When handling a group of records, whether they are clients or suppliers, you have the ability to perform specific actions on multiple records simultaneously.

Customizing List Settings

You can tailor the appearance and content of lists on the Customers, Vendors, and Employees pages to suit your preferences. This includes deciding whether to display or conceal details such as street addresses, attachments, emails, and phone numbers. You can also opt to include or exclude inactive entries from the list.

Moreover, you have the flexibility to determine the number of entries shown on each page and adjust the column width for those entries.

Depending on the specific list you're working with, you may have the option to show or hide particular elements. For example, you can choose to reveal or hide address information for customers and vendors, while this option may not apply to employees or contractors.

To access the respective list settings:

1. Select the appropriate link from the Navigation bar (Sales, Expenses, or Employees).

2. Click the gear icon located above the "Action" column at the right side of the page to modify the list's displayed data. You can select or deselect checkboxes to show or hide information.

3. After making your changes, click outside of the list.

It's advisable to click in the open space at the bottom of the Navigation bar when exiting the list to avoid accidentally leaving the current page.

Accessing Additional Lists

You can access various lists by selecting the gear symbol for "Settings" in the heading. "Lists" is one of the categories you'll find.

To view more lists:

1. Click "All Lists" under the "Lists" category.

This action will lead you to a page containing a variety of lists, including Recurring Transactions, Product Categories, Custom Form Styles, Payment Methods, Terms, Attachments, and the Chart of Accounts, Products, and Services.

You can easily return to the list view by selecting "All Lists" from the breadcrumb navigation below the title after opening any list in full table format. This course will begin with an overview of the recurring transactions list.

Importing Customers and Vendors

Before importing customer data into QuickBooks, it's crucial to understand the formatting requirements and file size restrictions to ensure a smooth data import process.

Here are some key considerations:

- File sizes have limitations, with a maximum import file size of 1,000 rows or 2MB for Excel and Outlook. For larger files, you'll need to split the data and perform multiple imports.

- Incorrect imports can cause issues, and re-importing a file after an improper import won't replace your customer list.

To avoid duplicates, remove incorrectly imported customers before re-importing the file.

- Sub-account imports are not supported. Prior to importing, convert subaccounts to parent accounts, and reverse the conversion after the import is completed.

- Only one email address is allowed during the QuickBooks import process, although additional email addresses can be added afterward.

- All data must have unique names. Each entry in the "Name" box must be distinct, and customer names cannot be the same.

For Excel Customer Lists:

To ensure the correct data is imported into the appropriate fields, confirm that your Excel customer spreadsheet is correctly formatted and mapped. Follow these steps:

1. Review the headers: Ensure the column headers in the spreadsheet's first row match the customer information, such as "Name," "Email," and "Mobile Number."

2. Fill in the sheet: Add contact information to a new spreadsheet if you're creating one. Leave any columns without data blank.

3. Save the Excel workbook: Keep track of the file's location and save it as an XLS or XLSX file, as the information you import should correspond to QuickBooks' invoicing data.

Here are the steps to import customers from Gmail to QuickBooks Online:

Method 1: Linking Gmail Contacts

1. Log in to QuickBooks Online.

2. Click on the "Settings" icon (the gear icon).

3. Select "Import Data."

4. Choose "Customers."

5. Navigate to the "Select a CSV or Excel file to upload" box and click "Browse."

6. Locate your Excel spreadsheet and click "Open."

7. Select "Next."

8. Check for any data warnings. A checkmark indicates comprehensive data. Click "Next."

9. Make necessary adjustments to the information if needed and click "Import."

Method 2: Importing Customers from Gmail

1. Sign in to your Gmail Account.

2. Click the "Contacts" icon on the right side of the screen.

3. Open a new tab by clicking the square icon with a diagonal arrow (square with an arrow).

4. Pick the contacts you wish to export or proceed to the next step.

5. Select "Export" from the left menu.

6. Click "Selected Contacts" to export the selected contacts or "Contacts" to export all contacts.

7. Choose "Export as" and select "Google CSV."

8. Click "Export," and you'll find the file in your Downloads folder.

9. After that, log in to QuickBooks Online and take the following actions:

10. Click on "Settings."

11. Choose "Import Data."

12. Click on "Customers."

13. In the "Select a CSV or Excel file to upload" box, select "Browse."

14. Click "Open" after navigating to the Google CSV file you just downloaded.

15. Select "Next."

16. You'll notice a warning if any data is missing. A checkmark will be present if the data is comprehensive. Choose "Next."

17. Make necessary adjustments to the information if needed, and then click on "Import."

Importing Lists

If you've been running your business for a while, chances are you've compiled lists of clients and suppliers. If you have electronic records of these lists, you can save setup time in QuickBooks Online (QBO) by importing them.

You can move your list information from QuickBooks Desktop to your QBO free trial, which can help you get accustomed to QBO by using familiar list data. It's worth noting that importing list data is different from importing an entire QuickBooks Desktop company.

Keep in mind that you can't import your list of employees, as they are considered "people." However, if you're importing a QuickBooks Desktop company that includes employees, you can import those employees.

You can import list data from an Excel file or a CSV file, even if you haven't used QuickBooks Desktop before. Most software, including QuickBooks Desktop, allows you to export data in CSV format, which stands for comma-separated values.

Fortunately, Excel can handle and save CSV files, making it convenient to open a CSV file, make necessary edits in Excel, and then save the updated CSV file. Alternatively, you can make updates to the file and save it as an Excel 97-2003 workbook.

To successfully import data into QBO from a CSV file or Excel workbook, your data must follow a specific format. The good news is that QBO offers the option to download a sample Excel file to see the required format for importing list data. You can use this sample as a template for setting up your own data.

The following actions assume that you already have Excel set up on your computer. If you don't have Excel, you can use Excel Mobile, a free app from Microsoft. To use Excel Mobile, you'll need to sign in with your Microsoft account email and password to make modifications to your files.

The steps below explain how to download and view the example file for suppliers:

1. After clicking "Expenses" in the Navigation bar, the Vendors page will appear.

2. In the top right corner of the screen, click the down arrow next to the "New Vendor" icon.

3. Select "Import Vendors."

4. Choose the link for "Download a Sample File." Clicking the link will trigger QBO to download the sample file and display a button for it in the Windows taskbar, assuming you're using Chrome.

5. Click on the button for the sample file located in the Windows taskbar.

6. Scroll to the right to review the file's content and the data stored in each column.

7. Use the example file as a model to structure your own data file. If you've been using QuickBooks Desktop, you can export your lists

to CSV or Excel files. For more information on this, consult QuickBooks Desktop Help.

Matching the headings in your data file to those in the sample data file will help ensure a smoother data import process. Remember that your data file should not exceed 2MB in size or contain more than 1,000 rows.

Also, be sure to save your data file as a CSV (comma-delimited) file or an Excel 97-2003 workbook.

Once you've prepared an Excel or CSV file containing your list data, you can proceed to import it. Follow these steps:

8. Make sure your data file is not open.

9. Access the "import vendors" or "import customers" page.

10. Click the "Browse" button.

11. Navigate to the folder where you've saved the file containing your list information.

12. Select "Open" after choosing the file. QBO will update the name of the file you've selected on the Import Vendors page.

13. Click "Next." QBO will upload your file and display the "Map Data" panel.

14. Check if the fields in your data file match up correctly with those in QBO. Open the list box next to each QBO field name as needed and compare it to the labels in your data file.

15. In the bottom right corner of the screen, click "Next." QBO will display the records it has located.

16. Verify the accuracy of the data in the records that QBO offers for import. You can change the content of any field by clicking on it and entering new data. Additionally, you can uncheck any row to prevent QBO from importing the data in that row.

17. Once you are certain the data is accurate, click the "Import" icon in the lower right corner of the screen.

If the "Import" button is grayed out and unavailable, it means that a portion of the data cannot be imported.

To identify the data that cannot be imported, look for a field highlighted in red. If the issue is unclear, consider seeking assistance from Intuit Support.

After importing the data, QBO will notify users of the number of records imported with a message. The relevant page will display the list you imported.

How to Export Lists to Excel or Google Sheets

If you wish to export your client or supplier lists to Excel, I assume you have Excel already installed on your computer, as it makes the process more convenient. However, if you don't have Excel, you can use the free mobile version of Excel.

To access either the Customers page or the Vendors page:

Choose the relevant link from the Navigation bar (Sales or Expenses). In this example, I'll select the Vendors page. You'll notice three buttons on the right side of the page, located just above the Action column. Click the middle button to export the list to an Excel file. If you're using Chrome, a button for the file will appear at the bottom of the screen.

When you click the button at the bottom of the screen, Excel will open the file. You can make modifications if you choose to. If you're using Excel mobile, you must sign in with your Microsoft account to make edits.

Introducing Spreadsheet Sync

You can synchronize Excel with your QuickBooks Online Advanced account using the Spreadsheet Sync feature, allowing you to:

Extract data from QuickBooks Online Advanced, edit it in an Excel file, and then update it.

Utilize the list templates in Spreadsheet Sync to create new data for QuickBooks Online Advanced.

Generate custom reports and keep them up-to-date with the latest information from QuickBooks Online Advanced.

Please note that only QuickBooks Online Advanced admin users can open and manage Spreadsheet Sync.

You can access Spreadsheet Sync in a few different ways when using QuickBooks Online Advanced:

Click on the Settings icon.

In the dropdown menu, select "Spreadsheet Sync."

From the side navigation panel, go to Reports.

Click on the caret icon near "Create new report" in the upper right corner and then select "Spreadsheet."

Open Spreadsheet Sync.

Installing the Spreadsheet Sync Add-In

To open Spreadsheet Sync from within Excel:

Click on "Launch Add-In Spreadsheet Sync" in the Excel navigation bar.

Choose "Sign in."

Enter your QuickBooks Online user ID in the task panel and click "Sign in."

- Insert your password and click on "Continue."

Managing List Records with Spreadsheet Sync

To extract company data into a spreadsheet:

- If your QuickBooks Online Advanced account administrator has assigned you to only one company, that company will appear in the "Please pick your company" dropdown.

- If you have been granted access to multiple companies, go to Company settings in the Spreadsheet Sync toolbar and click "Add new" to begin using the data of that specific company.

- Please note that adding companies to Spreadsheet Sync and configuring user permissions require access to QuickBooks Online Advanced.

To create a spreadsheet report:

- Click on "Build Reports" in the toolbar.

- Start by selecting the Company or Group data you want to download, and then choose the data source and the report or data table template you wish to use.

To edit or add data to your QuickBooks Online Advanced account:

- Click "Manage Records" in the toolbar.

- Under the "Records to create or edit" menu, select a list template, and then choose the Company or Group data you want to modify or add to.

Uninstalling Spreadsheet Sync

To discontinue using Spreadsheet Sync, simply sign out:

- Click "Launch Add-In Spreadsheet Sync" in the Excel navigation bar.

- Choose "Sign out."

This chapter focuses on the customer, the heart of the business, along with staff and vendors. You should be familiar with the concepts covered in the previous chapter, including creating and sorting records, working with different list types in QBO, importing data from various sources, and utilizing Spreadsheet Sync.

This chapter provides a wealth of information, so it's recommended to study and practice diligently.

CHAPTER 4

A Special Guide to Manageing Sales Tax, Services, and Inventory on QuickBooks

In QuickBooks Online, you have all the essential tools to efficiently oversee your inventory.

You can effortlessly track inventory levels, receive timely replenishment reminders, and gain valuable insights into your purchasing and sales patterns. Furthermore, you can easily include non-inventory items and services in your sales forms.

To maintain the accuracy of your records, it's essential to input all purchases and sales as inventory in QuickBooks. The software will then handle adjustments to your inventory levels as you go about your business tasks. Once your inventory setup is complete, managing inventory and adding items to your sales forms becomes a straightforward process.

Setting Up Sales Tax

Setting up sales tax in QuickBooks Online is a straightforward process thanks to a user-friendly wizard. The setup wizard will guide you through the steps, asking for basic information like your address and whether you're required to charge sales tax outside of your state.

For a smoother experience, it's recommended to configure your sales tax settings before setting up items. This is because QuickBooks Online utilizes the sales tax information you provide when configuring your products. Failing to set up sales taxes initially might necessitate revisiting each item individually to ensure tax compliance.

For businesses using the accrual basis of accounting, QuickBooks Online can automatically track and remit sales tax. Additionally, if your QuickBooks Online company operates on an accrual basis, the software will automatically calculate sales tax for your transactions.

If your company typically uses the cash basis of accounting, transitioning to the accrual method temporarily is necessary for setting up sales tax in QuickBooks Online.

Here's a step-by-step guide:

1. Click on the "Settings" (gear) icon and select "Account and Settings" > "Advanced."

After configuring these settings, you can proceed to add sales tax and then revert to the cash accounting method. It's essential to note that the Sales Tax Center will track your sales tax obligations on an accrual basis. However, you can rely on the Sales Tax Liability reports to determine the precise amount of sales tax to be remitted.

When you first access the sales tax setup in QuickBooks Online, the system will guide you through the process. Here's what you need to do:

1. Select "Taxes."

2. From the menu, choose "Setup Sales Tax."

The setup wizard will inquire about your company's address, which is essential for sales tax compliance. If you've previously entered your company's address in QuickBooks Online, it will be displayed for your verification.

1. If your address is accurate, click "Next."

The wizard will also inquire whether you need to charge sales tax in states other than your home state. You can respond with either "No" or "Yes." If you select "Yes," you'll be prompted to specify the additional states where you're required to charge sales tax. Then, click "Next."

QuickBooks Online will then inquire about your current tax year's start date, the frequency of your sales tax return filing, and the date you first began collecting sales tax for your taxing authority.

You also have the flexibility to add and modify tax agencies, rates, and settings within the Sales Tax Center.

Adding tax rates and agencies in QuickBooks Online is a straightforward process.

Here are the steps to do it:

1. Go to "Taxes" and click on "Sales tax."

2. Under the "Related Tasks" list on the right-hand side, click on "Add/edit tax rates and agencies."

3. Click on "New" and choose whether you want to set up a single tax rate or a combined tax rate.

4. Provide the necessary details, which include the tax's name, the agency to which you make payments, and the rate's percentage. If you only have one rate for one agency, enter that rate.

5. Click "Save" to confirm.

When you need to manage sales tax for multiple taxing authorities, you can create a combined tax rate. This is especially useful if you have to report and pay sales tax to different government entities, such as state, county, and city.

Here's how to add a combined tax rate:

1. Go to "Taxes" and click on "Sales tax."

2. Under the "Related Tasks" list on the right, choose "Add/edit tax rates and agencies."

3. Click "New."

4. Select "Combined tax rate."

5. Enter a name for the combined rate and specify the different sales tax components.

6. If necessary, choose "Add Another Component" to include additional rates.

7. Click "Save" to confirm.

Once you've added a combined tax rate, the following will occur:

- The list of Sales Tax Rates and Agencies will include the new rate.

- You can select the new combined rate in forms like invoices.

- The Sales Tax Owing list in the Sales Tax Center allows you to see the amounts owed to each tax agency.

- The Sales Tax Liability report is accessible to help you manage your sales tax obligations effectively.

Editing a tax rate or agency's name, modifying sales tax center filters, and adjusting sales tax settings in QuickBooks Online is a straightforward process.

Here's how to perform these tasks:

Editing a Tax Rate:

When you need to make changes to a tax rate, keep in mind the following:

- You can edit a sales tax rate if necessary.

- You can edit component rates individually.

- Editing a combined rate requires changes to its component rates.

Follow these steps to edit a tax rate:

1. Navigate to "Taxes," then click on "Sales tax."

2. Under the "Related Tasks" list on the right-hand side, choose "Add/edit tax rates and agencies."

3. Click on the rate you want to change and select "Edit."

4. Enter the new rate, and if necessary, update the agency's name.

5. Click the "Save" button to confirm.

After completing these steps, the following outcomes may occur:

- The new rate applies to new transactions.

- The new rate is applied to new transactions with past dates.

- The previous rate is no longer usable after editing.

- Transactions made at the older rate remain valid unless you explicitly select a different sales tax rate when editing the transaction.

- New transactions using recurring templates that employ the modified component are subject to the new rate, while earlier rates and transactions completed with the template remain unaffected.

- Reports provide information on both the rates before and after editing.

Editing the Name of a Tax Agency:

When changing the name of a tax agency, remember the following:

- The Tax Rate field cannot be modified.

- Deactivate the current tax name and rate if the rate needs to change.

- Create a new tax with the desired rate afterward.

To edit the name of a tax agency, follow these steps:

1. Go to "Taxes" and click on "Sales Tax."

2. Below the name of the agency you wish to edit, click on "Rename."

3. Enter the new name, then click "Save."

Changing Sales Tax Center Filters:

To modify the filters in the Sales Tax Center, follow these steps:

1. Navigate to "Taxes" and click on "Sales tax."

2. Select your preferred filter from the "Start of Year" and "Accounting Basis" drop-down menu.

Editing Sales Tax Settings:

To enable or disable sales tax and adjust settings, use the following steps:

1. Navigate to "Taxes" and click on "Sales tax."

2. Under the "Related Tasks" list on the right-hand side, click on "Edit sales tax settings."

3. Choose "Yes" if you charge sales tax and configure the options provided.

4. If you don't charge sales tax, choose "No." If you've applied sales tax to previous transactions, you must first process that before disabling sales tax.

5. Click "Save" to confirm the changes.

To deactivate a tax rate, follow these steps:

1. Go to "Taxes," then click on "Sales tax."

2. Under the "Related Tasks" list on the right-hand side, choose "Add/edit tax rates and agencies."

3. Select the tax rate name you want to deactivate.

4. Click "Deactivate."

5. Confirm your choice by clicking "Continue."

Managing Sales Tax, Services, and Inventory

With QuickBooks Online, you have all the necessary tools to efficiently manage your inventory. You can easily track your inventory, receive timely reminders for restocking, and gain valuable insights into your sales and purchases. Additionally, you can also include non-inventory goods and services on your sales forms.

To ensure accurate tracking, it's essential to enter all purchases and sales as inventory items in QuickBooks. Once set up, QuickBooks will automatically adjust your inventory levels as you make sales and purchases, making the process seamless.

Setting Up Sales Tax

Setting up sales tax in QuickBooks is a straightforward process. QuickBooks guides you through it, asking for basic information such as your business address and whether you need to charge sales tax outside your state. It's advisable to set up sales taxes before adding items to ensure that the tax data is correctly applied. If you set up products first and then the sales taxes, you may need to go back and make each item tax-deductible.

For businesses using the accrual accounting method, QuickBooks automatically tracks and submits sales tax. If your accounting basis is set to accrual, QuickBooks calculates sales tax on transactions automatically.

If your company operates on a cash basis, you can temporarily switch to the accrual method to set up sales tax, and then switch back to cash accounting.

To set up sales tax, follow these steps:

1. Click on "Settings (gear) > Account and Settings > Advanced."

Once you've set up sales tax, you can easily manage and edit tax rates and agencies.

Adding Tax Rates and Agencies

To add tax rates and agencies in QuickBooks:

1. Navigate to "Taxes" and click on "Sales tax."

2. Under "Related Tasks" on the right side, select "Add/edit tax rates and agencies."

3. Click "New" and choose either a single or combined tax rate.

4. Enter the tax name, the agency you pay, and the rate percentage. If you pay one rate to one agency, use that rate.

5. Click "Save."

Adding a Combined Rate

If you need to track sales tax for multiple taxing authorities, you can set up a combined tax rate. Here's how:

1. Navigate to "Taxes" and click on "Sales tax."

2. Under "Related Tasks," select "Add/edit tax rates and agencies."

3. Click "New."

4. Choose "Combined tax rate."

5. Enter a name for the combined rate and specify the different sales tax components.

6. If needed, choose "Add Another Component" to include more than two rates.

7. Click "Save."

Editing a Tax Rate

To edit a tax rate, follow these steps:

1. Navigate to "Taxes" and click on "Sales tax."

2. Under "Related Tasks," select "Add/edit tax rates and agencies."

3. Click on the rate you want to change, then choose "Edit."

4. Enter the new rate, and change the agency's name if necessary.

5. Click "Save."

Deactivating a Tax Rate

If you need to deactivate a tax rate, here's what you should do:

1. Go to "Taxes" and click on "Sales tax."

2. Under "Related Tasks," select "Add/edit tax rates and agencies."

3. Pick a tax rate name and click on "Deactivate."

4. Click "Continue."

Understanding Sales Tax Liability

Sales tax liability refers to the money that businesses must collect from customers and remit to federal, state, and municipal taxing bodies. In QuickBooks, you can track your sales tax obligations using a sales tax liability report, which lists the tax amounts paid to tax authorities and the tax collected.

Different locations may have various types or classifications of sales tax due to state and municipal governments' varying roles in collecting sales tax.

Different sales tax scenarios include:

1. Food: Some states don't tax food for domestic use, while others charge a reduced sales tax rate on food. Local governments typically follow federal or state exemptions on food taxation.

2. Vehicles: Most states charge sales tax on vehicles purchased within their jurisdiction, with tax rates determined by the buyer's residence.

3. Medical Appliances: Sales tax on medical items depends on the state. Prescription medications are usually tax-exempt, while non-prescription medicines and medical equipment may be taxed.

4. General Merchandise: Most states apply sales tax to everyday items like soda, sweets, restaurant food, computer software, and hygiene products.

Enabling the Automated Sales Tax Feature

QuickBooks offers an automated sales tax feature to streamline your tax management.

Here's how to set it up:

1. Go to "Taxes" and click on "Sales tax."

2. Under "Related Tasks," select "Edit sales tax settings."

3. Choose "Yes" if you charge sales tax. Configure the default tax rate and other options.

4. If you don't charge sales tax, select "No." You'll need to address any previous transactions with sales tax first.

5. Click "Save."

Managing sales tax in QuickBooks is essential for accurate record-keeping and tax compliance. QuickBooks Online makes it easier for businesses to handle their sales tax responsibilities efficiently.

Converting Sales Tax from QuickBooks Desktop

When transitioning from QuickBooks Desktop to QuickBooks Online, it's essential to be aware that sales tax doesn't transfer seamlessly. Some taxes may import as list balances, while others become journal entries. QuickBooks Online uses sales tax accounts that are separate from those in QuickBooks Desktop. Therefore, be prepared for some variations in sales tax when importing your company file.

Sales tax is a critical component of your financial records, and ensuring its accurate management is vital for maintaining your business's financial health.

Reordering Inventory Items in QuickBooks Online

Managing your inventory in QuickBooks Online is essential to keep track of supplies and items. When your inventory reaches a low point, it's crucial to reorder items promptly.

Here's how you can efficiently manage your inventory:

Step 1: Check Your Stock Levels

Begin by checking if you have low stock or items that are out of stock. QuickBooks Online provides alerts to help you identify items that need to be reordered urgently.

1. Go to "Get paid & pay" or "Sales" and select "Products and services."

2. At the top, you can easily spot low-stock or out-of-stock items. Select "Low stock" or "Out of stock" to view the items falling into these categories.

QuickBooks uses reorder points to determine when items should be reordered.

If your existing products lack reorder points, you can add them when you add new products or update existing ones.

Step 2: Create and Send a Purchase Order

Once you've identified the items you need to reorder, the next step is to inform your suppliers by sending a purchase order.

1. Go to "Get paid & pay" or "Sales" and select "Products and services."

2. Choose "Out of Stock" or "Low Stock." If you need to reorder both low-stock and out-of-stock items from the same source, use none of the top filters.

3. Select the items you wish to reorder from the list.

4. Choose "Batch activities," and then select "Reorder." This generates a purchase order for a single vendor.

5. Fill out the purchase order with the necessary details and add any additional products that need to be replenished.

6. Select "Send and save."

Step 3: Track Your Vendor Order

After creating a purchase order, you'll need to track your vendor's order. You can do this in one of two ways:

1. If you intend to pay your vendor in the future, create a bill from the purchase order.

2. If you made an immediate payment to the vendor, make a check or an expenditure from the purchase order.

Tracking your vendor order in QuickBooks updates the quantity on hand as you receive items, helping you keep accurate inventory records.

Creating Inventory Adjustment Transactions

Sometimes, you may find that your actual inventory quantity doesn't match what's recorded in QuickBooks. QuickBooks Online Plus and Advanced users can manually adjust an item's quantity to reflect the actual stock levels.

Here's how to do it:

1. Click on "New."

2. Choose "Inventory quantity adjustment."

3. Enter the adjustment date.

4. Select the appropriate account from the "Inventory adjustment account" drop-down.

5. In the Product section, choose the desired products. The description and available quantity are automatically filled in.

6. Enter the new quantity or changes for each item.

7. Specify the adjustment details in the Memo section.

8. When you're done, select "Save and close."

By creating inventory adjustments, you can maintain accurate inventory records and ensure that your stock levels in QuickBooks match the actual quantities on hand.

Organizing Categories

In QuickBooks, you have the option to use categories instead of individual items for subscriptions that involve sub-items. This doesn't apply to users who switched from QuickBooks Desktop.

Categories can be utilized to classify the products you sell, offering a better understanding of your customers' preferences. It's important to note that categories don't impact your financial or accounting reports, and transactions cannot be assigned categories.

You can add categories when adding products or set them up in advance to use later.

Here's how:

1. Go to the Products and Services list page under "Get paid & pay" or "Sales."

2. If you prefer to set up categories beforehand, select "Manage Categories" from the More menu.

3. To add a new category, click the "New Category" button on the Product Categories page. Enter the category name in the Category Information panel on the right side of your screen.

If the new category is a subcategory of an existing one, check the "Is a Sub-Category" box and choose the parent category's name. Finally, click "Save" at the bottom of the screen.

You can edit or remove existing categories by clicking the "Edit" link next to them on the Product Categories page.

Changing Item Types

You have the flexibility to change the item type for services or non-inventory items individually or for multiple products simultaneously. However, there are specific limitations when it comes to changing item types. You can only change from:

- Non-inventory and Service items to Inventory items.

- Service items to Non-inventory items.

- Non-inventory items to service items.

Multiple changes occur when switching between service and non-inventory items, while you can only change one item at a time when converting service or non-inventory items to inventory items. Bundles, which consist of predefined items, cannot be changed into any other item type.

If the item type of a bundled item changes, QuickBooks Online automatically updates the bundle with the new information.

To change the item type of any individual item, follow these steps:

1. Click "Edit" in the Action column of the Products and Services list.

2. In the Product/Service detail panel, click the "Change Type" link above the item's name.

3. Select the new item type, and QuickBooks Online updates the Product/Service Information panel accordingly.

After making any necessary adjustments, click "Save and Close."

Streamlining Your Invoicing Process

In QuickBooks Online, you can create and send invoices to notify customers of amounts owed for items or services.

When generating invoices in QuickBooks Online, you have the option to send them via email or USPS.

For those who use Google Calendar, the "Invoice with Google Calendar" tool, available in the Intuit App Center, simplifies the process of transferring event details and descriptions from your Google Calendar to a QuickBooks Online invoice.

Here's how to use it:

Open a QuickBooks Online invoice form and click the Google Calendar icon, which appears on the form after enabling the integration between your Google Calendar and QuickBooks Online.

You can set search criteria using a panel on the right side of the invoice form. Choose a Google Calendar, a time frame, and a search term.

When you opt to add events to the invoice, QuickBooks Online imports event details from your Google Calendar, including the event title, description, hours worked, and date, eliminating the need for duplicate data entry.

You can also utilize the QuickBooks Invoicing for Gmail add-on to send invoices directly from Gmail and allow clients to make online payments. This software, available through QuickBooks Labs, charges per transaction but doesn't require a monthly subscription cost.

Managing Products and Services via Spreadsheet Integration

You can efficiently manage your products and services in QuickBooks by importing data from a spreadsheet or manually adding items. Importing via a spreadsheet is the quickest method to populate your QuickBooks with all your products and services.

Here's how:

1. Navigate to "Sales" in the left menu. Choose the "Products and Services" sub-tab, then click "Import."

2. Examine the sample Excel worksheet that you can download.

3. Organize your spreadsheet so that the column names and order match those in the sample file. Once ready, return to the Import screen, click "Browse," and upload your file.

4. Link each QuickBooks field to a specific column in your Excel workbook. Data from the chosen column will be imported into the selected QuickBooks field.

5. Verify your data to ensure everything is accurately mapped and make any necessary corrections. When finished, click "Import."

With the extensive capabilities that QuickBooks Online offers, you may feel like you've discovered a valuable tool. You've learned about sales tax, its configuration in QuickBooks Online, sales tax responsibility, and how to automate the sales tax feature. Additionally, you've learned how to transition your valuable sales data to QuickBooks Online. You should also be familiar with the new Nexus feature, client list auditing, product and service management, and price rule application. Make sure you review all the activities below, practice, and give them a try.

CHAPTER 5

Invoicing Customers and Managing Payments

This chapter marks the exciting part of business – raising capital, the most enjoyable aspect for any businessperson. It covers various aspects of sales transactions, allowing you to effectively manage your business finances.

Here's a brief overview:

Getting Acquainted with Sales Transactions

You can easily access sales transaction details, including open and paid invoices, on the Sales page. This page not only provides an overview but also allows you to create and modify sales transactions. To access it:

- Navigate to "Bookkeeping," select "Transactions," and click "All Sales." Alternatively, go to "Sales" and choose "All Sales."

View Transaction and Invoice Status Effortlessly

The Money Bar, a vital element on the Sales page, displays a quick summary of open and recently paid invoices, as well as the status and amounts of your sales transactions. It also shows unbilled fees, charges, time activities, or estimates.

The list of transactions includes estimates, invoices, sales receipts, payments, credit memos, delayed charges (QuickBooks Online Plus, Advanced, and Essentials only), and billable time activities (QuickBooks Online Plus and Advanced only).

This list makes it simple to track transaction statuses like Open, Closed, Paid, Partially Paid, or Overdue.

Customize the list to view only the relevant data by using filters, adjust columns to display necessary information, or export lists to Microsoft Excel for versatile data handling.

Remember that the default view for all transactions is set to "365 days," so invoices older than this will not appear in the Invoices page.

Effortless Management of Sales Transactions

Managing sales transactions from the Sales page is straightforward:

- Create new invoices, payments, sales receipts, estimates, credit memos, delayed charges, and billable time activities by selecting from the New Transaction dropdown menu.

- Perform various actions on transactions, such as receiving payments, printing transactions, sending them, or even deleting, invalidating, or copying them.

- Update the status of estimates and make additional entries for customers, including charges, time activities, and credits (QuickBooks Online Plus, Advanced, and Essentials only).

Creating Invoices

To ensure you get paid for your products or services in the future, sending an invoice is essential. Here's how to create and send invoices:

Step 1: Create and Send an Invoice

Using the traditional experience:

1. Click "New."

2. Choose "Invoice."

3. Select a customer from the Customer dropdown menu and ensure all information, including the email address, is accurate.

4. Check the invoice's date and change the due date if needed.

5. Choose a product or service from the Product/Service column.

6. Enter quantity, rate, and amount changes if necessary.

7. Enable tax if required.

8. To save or distribute the invoice, you have several options:

- Choose "Save and Send" when ready to email the invoice, edit the email if necessary, and click "Send and Close."

- Select "Save and Close" to send the invoice at a later time.

- Choose "Save" to print a hard copy, then select "Print" or "Preview."

- Opt for "Save and Share a Link" to SMS your customer a link to their invoice.

Step 2: Review Unpaid Invoices

To manage your unpaid invoices and keep track of your accounts receivable, follow these steps:

- Go to "Get Paid & Pay" or "Sales & Costs" and select "Invoices" to review your invoices. Check the Status column to see where invoices stand in the sales process.

Step 3: Receive Payments for Invoices

If you use QuickBooks Payments, customers can conveniently pay their invoices via credit card or ACH transfer, with transactions automatically recorded.

Payments made through an external platform can also be monitored within QuickBooks.

How to Record Customer Payments

After receiving a payment from a customer, you'll need to record it in QBO. Here are several options for accessing the Receive Payment window:

1. From the Sales Transactions list, find the invoice for which you want to record a payment, then click "Receive Payment" in the Action column.

2. On the Sales Transactions page, click the "New Transaction" button and select "Payment."

3. Choose "Receive Payment" from the Create menu.

4. Select "Projects," pick the project you're working on, and click "Add to Project."

If you choose the first option, QBO will open the Receive Payment window with the details of the selected invoice, including a suggested payment amount.

With the second or third approach, you'll see a blank Receive Payment window. Once you've chosen a customer, the "Outstanding Transactions" section at the bottom of the window will display all the customer's open bills.

Here's how to record the payment:

- Pick a payment method at the top of the screen.

- Choose the account where you want QBO to deposit the customer's payment.

- Enter the amount received in the "Amount Received" column.

- Check the box next to each invoice that has been paid with the customer's payment in the "Outstanding Transactions" section.

Understanding the Payments to Deposit Account

Payments received through credit cards and ACH using QuickBooks Payments are deposited into an external bank account, often referred to as your "payments account." You can think of this as the account where you collect payments. Keep in mind that you can use only one account to collect payments at a time.

Changing Your Payments Acount

To update your payments account, follow these steps based on your QuickBooks product:

For Standard Deposits:

1. Log in to QuickBooks Online using a web browser.

2. Select "Account and Settings" from the "Settings" menu.

3. Click on the "Payments" tab.

4. Under "Standard Deposits" in the "Deposits" section, select "Change bank."

5. Choose "Create a new bank account" to modify your bank account details.

6. Provide the routing number and account number.

7. Click "Save" when you're ready.

8. Double-check the bank account information before submitting your request.

For Instant Deposits:

1. In the "Settings" menu, choose "Account and Settings."

2. Navigate to the "Deposit accounts" section under the "Payments" tab.

3. Select "Change" to modify your instant deposit information. If you switch from your personal debit card to your QuickBooks Cash debit card, select the 0% fee option.

4. Click "Save" and then "Done" when finished.

Customer payments from online invoicing and other sources will be deposited into the new account by QuickBooks. This change does not affect how payments are categorized in your chart of accounts; it only updates the bank account QuickBooks uses for depositing funds.

Recording Invoice Payments

When your clients plan to pay you for your goods or services at a later date, you need to create and send invoices. To maintain accurate accounts, it's crucial to record customer payments and link them to the corresponding invoices.

Please note that if you use QuickBooks Payments for processing payments, the accounting is handled for you.

QuickBooks automatically processes the funds and associates them with the relevant account when your client pays the invoice.

To mark an invoice as paid, you must record the customer's payment after processing it in QuickBooks. If you don't do this, the invoice will remain open and show as underpaid in your records.

An invoice can be paid in full or in part, and QuickBooks keeps track of any remaining unpaid amounts.

For recording a payment for a single invoice:

1. Click on "+ New."

2. Select "Receive Payment."

3. Choose the customer's name from the Customer dropdown menu.

4. Pick the payment method from the Payment method dropdown.

5. Select the account where you want to deposit the funds from the "Deposit to" dropdown menu.

6. Check the box next to the invoice for which you are recording the payment in the "Outstanding Transactions" section.

7. If needed, enter the Memo and Reference number.

8. Click "Save and close."

For recording a partial payment for an invoice:

1. Click on "+ New."

2. Select "Receive Payment."

3. Choose the customer's name from the Customer dropdown menu.

4. Pick the payment method from the Payment method dropdown.

5. Select the account where you want to deposit the funds from the "Deposit to" dropdown menu.

6. Enter the customer's payment amount in the "Amount received" column.

7. Check the box next to the invoice for which you are recording the payment in the "Outstanding Transactions" section.

8. If needed, enter the Memo and Reference number.

9. Click "Save and close."

When recording partial payments, QuickBooks applies the payment to the invoice line items sequentially. Any additional payments are applied to the subsequent line items until the payment is completed.

For situations where you have more than one payment in a single deposit, you can use the "Undeposited Funds" account in QuickBooks.

This allows you to consolidate multiple payments into a single QuickBooks deposit transaction, which is especially useful when your bank combines several payments into one deposit.

Entering a Sales Receipt

In case you're using a different Point of Sale system or simply need to record overall daily sales quickly without sending individual invoices to customers, you can enter a single sales receipt in QuickBooks.

This helps save time while maintaining accurate income reports. Follow these step-by-step instructions:

Step 1: Create a customer for daily sales

1. Navigate to Customers by going to Get paid & pay or Sales.

2. Choose New customer.

3. Name the customer "Daily Sales."

4. Click Save.

Step 2: Set up accounts for daily sales

Ensure your accounting for daily sales is in order to maintain accurate income reporting.

1. Click the Gear icon on the Toolbar.

2. Select Chart of Accounts from the Your Company menu.

3. Click New in the top right corner.

4. Create the following accounts:

   - Income: Daily Sales

   - Payment Methods: Cash

   - Payment Methods: Check

   - Payment Methods: Visa/Mastercard

   - Payment Methods: American Express

   - Payment Methods: Overage/Underage

- Payment Methods: Discover

Step 3: Set up items for daily sales

Organize your items by creating a category named "Daily Sales."

1. Click the Gear icon on the Toolbar.

2. Select All Lists from the Lists menu.

3. Choose your preferred Product categories.

4. In the top right corner, select New Category.

5. Name the new category "Daily Sales."

6. Click Save.

Create the following items:

1. Click the Gear icon on the Toolbar.

2. Select Products and Services from the Lists section.

3. Click New in the top right corner.

4. Set up these items. Make sure to choose "Daily Sales" as the Category for each item.

Step 4: Create a daily sales template

This template will be used for tracking daily total sales.

1. Click the Gear icon on the Toolbar.

2. Select Recurring Transactions from the list.

3. Click New in the top right corner.

4. Choose Sales Receipt from the Transaction Type dropdown menu.

5. Ensure the Type is Unscheduled and name your template "Daily Sales."

6. Select "Daily Sales" as the customer.

7. Choose the following items in the Product/Service section:

- Daily Sales: Daily Sales Income

- Daily Sales: Cash

- Daily Sales: Check

- Daily Sales: Visa/Mastercard

- Daily Sales: American Express

- Daily Sales: Overage/Underage

- Daily Sales: Discover

8. Click Save template.

Step 5: Record your total daily sales

Your sales receipt template is now prepared for recording daily total sales.

1. Click the Gear icon on the Toolbar.

2. Select Recurring Transactions from the Lists menu.

3. Once you've found your template, choose Use from the Action menu.

4. Review the sample breakdown of total daily sales to understand how your sales receipt should appear.

Recording Bank Deposits

When you frequently make bank deposits that involve multiple payments from different sources,

QuickBooks allows you to combine these transactions into a single bank deposit record, which matches how your bank reports the deposit.

Follow these steps to record bank deposits in QuickBooks Online:

Step 1: Put transactions into the Undeposited Funds account

If you haven't already, gather any invoice payments and sales receipts you want to combine into the Undeposited Funds account.

This account acts as a holding area for transactions before they are deposited.

QuickBooks handles the processing and transfer of transactions to your accounts automatically.

While not required, using the Undeposited Funds account is helpful.

Step 2: Combine transactions in QuickBooks with a bank deposit

In QuickBooks, each bank deposit generates a unique record.

Create one deposit at a time for your deposit slips:

1. Click + New.

2. Choose Bank Deposit.

3. Select the account you wish to deposit the money into from the Account menu.

4. Tick the appropriate box for each transaction you want to combine.

5. Verify that the sum of the selected transactions matches the amount on your deposit slip, using it as a reference.

6. Choose Save and New or Save and Close.

Tracking Invoice Status and Receiving Payment with Schedule Pay

Schedule Pay encourages timely payments from your clients by allowing them to choose a due date when viewing the invoice. Clients can select any date for payment until the invoice's due date.

To set up Schedule Pay for your invoices, no further action is needed on your part as long as your invoices are configured to accept online payments.

Clients will see the Schedule Pay option when they click the Review and Pay button in their emailed invoice.

Please note that Schedule Pay won't work if:

- The invoice is Due on receipt.

- Your customer edits the payment amount.

- The main amount of the invoice is $50,000 or more.

You can also track the Schedule Pay status of your customers' invoices by following these steps:

1. Select Sales, then Invoices.

2. Locate the invoice for which you want to verify the payment status.

3. The activity tracker panel will appear when the status field on that invoice line is selected.

4. When the Payment Scheduled status appears below the invoice activity section, you know your customer has set up Schedule Pay.

Providing Refunds to Customers

Occasionally, situations arise where you need to refund money to a customer. In such cases, follow these steps:

- If a customer returns goods to you, send a credit memo.

- Alternatively, if you need to reimburse a customer for their payment, you can issue a refund receipt.

This might occur when a customer's goods arrive damaged, and they prefer a refund instead of placing another order.

Refunding a Customer's Deposit

If a customer paid you a down payment on an invoice but later canceled the deal and is entitled to a refund, you can process the refund and apply it to their credit. Here's how to refund the deposit and update your records in QuickBooks Online:

Step 1: Create a Credit Memo

1. Click on + New.

2. Select Credit Memo.

3. Choose the customer's name associated with the invoice.

4. In the Amount field, enter the total amount of the invoice, including the deposit.

5. Click Save.

Step 2: Issue a Refund Check

1. Click on + New.

2. Select Check.

3. In the Payee field, choose the customer.

4. Under Category Details, select Accounts Receivable from the Category menu.

5. Enter the total deposit amount in the Amount field.

6. Click Save and Close.

Step 3: Record the Payment

1. Click on + New.

2. Select Receive Payment.

3. Choose the customer's name linked to your invoice.

4. Ensure that the total credits match the credit memo and invoice mentioned in the Outstanding Transactions section.

5. Check the boxes next to the invoice and credit memo in the Outstanding Transactions section.

6. Click Save and Close.

By following these steps, you can efficiently process a refund for your customer and maintain accurate records in QuickBooks Online.

Handling Bad Debt

Dealing with bad debt is an essential financial process that ensures your books remain accurate even when you face unrecoverable debts.

Here's how to write off bad debt in QuickBooks:

Step 1: Review Aging Accounts Receivable

1. Generate an Accounts Receivable Aging Detail report.

- Access Reports from the Business overview menu or directly from the Reports section.

- Open the Accounts Receivable Aging Detail report.

- Identify the unpaid accounts receivables that should be written off as bad debt.

Step 2: Establish a Bad Debts Expense Account

1. Navigate to Settings and click on the chart of accounts.

2. Create a new account by clicking New in the upper right corner.

3. Choose Expenses as the Account Type.

4. Select Bad debts from the Detail Type menu.

5. Enter "Bad debts" in the Name field.

6. Click Save and Close.

Step 3: Create a Bad Debt Item

1. Go to Products and Services in the Settings menu.

2. Select New, then Non-inventory, from the upper right menu.

3. Name the item as "Bad debts" in the Name field.

4. Choose the Bad debts account from the Income account dropdown.

5. Click Save and Close.

Step 4: Generate a Credit Memo for Bad Debt

1. Click on + New.

2. Choose Credit Memo.

3. Select the customer from the Customer option.

4. Pick "Bad debts" from the Product/Service dropdown.

5. Enter the amount you want to deduct in the Amount column.

6. Include "Bad Debt" in the Message box on the statement.

7. Click Save and Close.

Step 5: Apply the Credit Memo to the Invoice

1. Click on + New.

2. Select Receive Payment from the Customers menu.

3. Choose the appropriate customer from the Customer selection.

4. Pick the invoice from the Outstanding Transactions list.

5. Select the credit memo from the Credits section.

6. Click Save and Close.

By following these steps, you can properly write off bad debt in QuickBooks, ensuring that your financial records remain up to date and accurate.

Paying Bills and Issuing Checks

While spending money may not be as exciting as earning it, managing bills is an essential aspect of financial responsibility. Let's explore the various transactions you can perform in QuickBooks Online (QBO) to meet your financial obligations.

If you've been in business for a while and have unpaid debts when you start using QBO, this chapter provides instructions on how to enter those bills, which can serve as valuable learning tools. Also, if you've recorded an opening bank account balance, ensure you enter checks that haven't yet cleared your bank into QBO.

Furthermore, input all checks written this year into QBO, even if they've cleared the bank, if you didn't record an opening bank account balance or entered a balance as of the previous year's December 31.

To record most expense-related transactions, navigate to the Expense Transactions page by selecting "Expenses" from the Navigation bar. Click the "New Transaction" button to choose the transaction type you wish to record.

Bill Payment Methods and Expenses:

When handling bills and expenses, consider the following methods:

1. Bill Payments:

- Use "Bill," and then "Pay bills" if you need to schedule bill payments for later.

- Choose "Check" or "Expense" based on whether the payment is for immediate or already settled expenses.

2. Bill Payments:

- Utilize "Pay bills" to settle a bill initially logged in QuickBooks. You can make payments using a credit card or print a check.

- When paying bills through "Pay Bills," the vendor amount is correctly reduced.

- Using "Check" or "Expense" might keep the bill showing as unpaid in your reports.

- For electronic bill payments, enter "EFT" in the Check No. field.

3. Checks or Expenses:

- Both "Check" and "Expense" transactions serve to record an expense and payment simultaneously.

- Checks and expenses are suitable for services or items paid instantly, while bills are for payables that will be settled at a later date.

- Record an expense as a "Check" instead of an "Expense" if you need to print a check.

- Use "Expense" for credit card payments.

- Whether you paid via EFT, you can input EFT details in the Check No. field.

For instance, if you purchased goods from Office Depot and made an immediate payment, record the transaction as a "Check" or "Expense." Since Office Depot does not owe any money, there is no need to enter and pay bills for this particular transaction.

Understanding Transaction Types

In QuickBooks, transaction types define the nature of a particular financial transaction, whether it's related to customers, bill payments, or bank transfers. When you input a transaction, you assign it a specific transaction code, helping QuickBooks categorize and report your financial activities.

Not all transaction types have corresponding codes, but you can filter and identify transactions in your reports by their transaction types.

Customer Transactions

At the heart of your business are customer transactions, and it's crucial to accurately record various transaction types. For instance, "RCPT" signifies a sales receipt, "ITEM RCPT" designates an item receipt (indicating receipt of items from a vendor without an invoice), and "TAXPMT" represents a sales tax payment. You use "STMTCHG" for statement charges billed to customers and "CREDMEM" for credit memos issued.

Bills and Invoices

To manage the money you owe or are owed, certain transaction types relate to transactions with vendors. "BILL" represents an unpaid vendor bill, "BILLPMT" indicates a paid vendor bill,

"BILLCRED" marks credit extended to you by a vendor, and "INV" signifies invoices issued to clients or vendors.

Checks and Credits

For those with employees, it's important to track payroll and business expenses. "CC" denotes a credit card charge, while "CC CRED" signifies a credit card credit, especially when returning purchases. "PAY CHK" is used for employee paychecks, and payroll tax and liability transactions are categorized under "LIAB CHK."

Generic Types

Several transaction categories don't involve direct interactions with other parties. "CHK" stands for checks, "DEP" represents bank deposits, and "TRANSFER" is used for transfers between two balance sheet accounts. "DISC" signifies discounts offered to customers or vendors for early payment, with QuickBooks automatically calculating the discount. Finally, "GENJRNL" is for general journal entries, used in situations where no other transaction type applies.

Additional Transaction Types

Purchase orders, estimates, pending assembly builds, and outstanding bills are further transaction types in QuickBooks. These types, without corresponding transaction codes, are typically used for internal reference or to manage finances and resources, rather than for posting to an account.

Entering an Expense

QuickBooks Online streamlines the process of recording business expenses alongside sales tracking. Entering expenses provides a more comprehensive view of your business and profits. When you've already made the payment, record an expense. For future payments, enter the expense as a bill.

The selection of the appropriate transaction type guides QuickBooks in recording each transaction accurately.

Here are the steps to record expenses in QuickBooks.

Recording an Expense

If you need to record a business expense in QuickBooks that has already been paid, simply follow these steps:

1. Click on "+ New" and then select "Expense."

2. In the "Payee" field, choose the vendor. Leave it blank if the transaction includes multiple petty cash expenditures.

3. Select the account used for covering the expense in the "Payment account" field.

4. Input the date of the expense in the "Payment date" section.

5. Choose your payment method from the "Payment method" area.

6. You can include a reference number or permit number for detailed tracking, although this is optional.

7. In the "Tags" area, enter a preferred label to categorize your money.

8. Fill in the "Category details" section with expense information. Choose the appropriate cost account from the "Category" selection and add a description. You can also specify individual goods and services in the "Item details" box to categorize the expense.

9. Add any applicable tax and the expense amount.

10. If you plan to bill the expense to a customer, check the "Billable" box and enter the customer's name in the "Customer" field.

11. Click "Save and close" to finish the process.

Writing a Check

To maintain your checking account records and manage your expenses effectively, you should record checks in QuickBooks. Whether you intend to print a new check or make a purchase with a handwritten check, here's how to create a check:

1. Select "+ New."

2. Choose "Check."

3. Pick the payee from the drop-down menu.

4. Specify the bank account from which the check will be drawn under the "Bank account" option.

5. Fill in the required checkboxes.

6. If you want to print the check immediately, use the "Print check" option. Alternatively, if you plan to print the check later, check the "Print later" box.

7. Complete the process by selecting "Save and close."

Entering a Bill

If you intend to pay for an expense at a later date, you should record it as a bill in QuickBooks. Here are the steps for entering an expense as a bill:

1. Choose "+ New."

2. Select "Bill."

3. Choose the vendor from the "Vendor" selection.

4. Specify the bill's terms from the "Terms" menu, including the anticipated payment date.

5. Enter the bill's date, due date, and bill number as indicated on the bill itself.

6. In the "Category details" section, provide the bill's details. Choose the appropriate cost account from the "Category" selection and add a description. You can also itemize the bill by specifying individual goods and services in the "Item details" area.

7. Include any applicable tax and the bill amount.

8. If you intend to bill the expense to a customer, select the "Billable" checkbox and enter the customer's name in the "Customer" field.

9. Once you've completed the necessary information, select "Save and close."

Uploading Bills from a Computer

If you want to upload bills from your computer, follow these steps:

1. Navigate to "Bills" by selecting "Get paid & pay."

2. Click on "Upload from the computer" from the "Add bill" dropdown menu.

3. You can upload files by dragging and dropping them into the upload window or by selecting the "Upload" option to choose files from your computer.

Paying Bills

To record a bill you've received from a vendor, use the following steps:

1. Click on "+ New."

2. Select "Bill."

3. Choose the vendor from the "Vendor" selection.

4. Specify the bill's terms, including the expected payment date.

5. Input the date, due date, and bill number as they appear on the bill.

6. In the "Category details" section, provide the bill's details, selecting the appropriate cost account from the "Category" selection and adding a description. You can also specify individual goods and services in the "Item details" area to itemize the bill.

7. Include any relevant tax and the bill amount.

8. If you plan to bill the expense to a customer, select the "Billable" checkbox and enter the customer's name in the "Customer" field.

9. Once you've entered all the necessary information, select "Save and close."

If you want to upload bills from your computer, follow these steps:

1. Navigate to "Bills" by selecting "Get paid & pay."

2. Click on "Upload from the computer" from the "Add bill" dropdown menu.

3. You can upload files by dragging and dropping them into the upload window or by selecting the "Upload" option to choose files from your computer.

Paying Multiple Bills at Once

To pay two or more bills at once, use the following steps:

1. Go to "Bills" under "Get paid & pay."

2. Select the "Unpaid" tab.

3. Choose "Schedule payment" next to the bill you want to pay and follow the on-screen instructions.

Writing a Check to Pay a Bill

To write a check to pay a bill, follow these steps:

1. Click on "+ New."

2. Choose "Check."

3. Select the vendor you paid from the "Payee" dropdown menu. This will display all their unpaid debts.

4. To add an open bill to the check, select "Add." If you can't see it, click the tiny arrow next to the amount. If you have vendor credit, you can also add it from the "Credits" section.

5. Specify the bank account used for the check payment under the "Bank/Credit account" selection.

6. Enter the check amount in the "Amount" field.

7. In the "Outstanding Transactions" section, select the invoices that the check payment covers. If multiple bills are involved, select the checkboxes next to the bills and specify different amounts in the "Payment" column for each bill.

8. Once done, click "Save."

Recording Vendor Credits and Refunds

How you handle your purchases affects how you record vendor credits. Here are the steps to record vendor credits, apply them to bills, and manage refunds:

Recording a Vendor Credit

If you use bills to track expenses, follow these instructions to ensure that the credit is correctly applied to the vendor's expense account:

1. Click on "+ New."

2. Select "Receive vendor credit" or "Vendor credit."

3. Choose the relevant vendor from the "Vendor" dropdown menu.

4. Depending on your method of expense tracking, enter either the "Category" data or "Item details." This typically represents the category, item, or service for which you are receiving credit.

5. Click "Save and close."

Applying Vendor Credits Against Bills

Vendor credits can be applied to pay any current or upcoming invoices. Here's how to utilize the credit when needed:

1. Click on "+ New."

2. Alternatively, choose to "Pay a bill."

3. Select a bill for the vendor from the list. The "Credit Applied" section will show the available credit.

4. Fill out the remaining fields as usual.

Recording Vendor Refund Checks and Payments

When a vendor sends you a refund check for a bill that has already been paid, you should follow these steps:

For Deposits of Vendor Checks:

1. Go to the "Banking" menu and select "Make Deposits."

2. If the "Payments to Deposit" window appears, click "OK."

3. In the "Make Deposits" window, choose the vendor who sent you the refund from the "Received" drop-down menu.

4. Select the appropriate "Accounts Payable" account from the "From Account" drop-down menu.

5. Enter the exact amount of the vendor check in the "Amount" column.

6. Optionally, include a memo, check number, payment method, and class.

7. Click "Save & Close."

For Bill Credits:

1. Select "Enter Bills" from the "Vendors" menu.

2. Choose the "Credit" radio button to record the return of items.

3. Enter the vendor's name.

4. Under the "Expenses" tab, enter the accounts from the original bill.

5. Specify the correct amounts for each account in the "Amount" column (amounts may need to be prorated).

6. Click "Save and Close."

Linking the Deposit to the Bill Credit:

1. Choose "Pay Bills" from the "Vendors" menu.

2. Ensure that the deposit amount matches the vendor check.

3. Apply the Bill Credit you created earlier by selecting "Set Credits," then click "Done."

4. After selecting "Pay Selected Bills," click "Done" once again.

For Deposits of Vendor Checks for Returned Inventory Items:

1. Follow the same steps as mentioned for depositing vendor checks.

2. For Bill Credits, select "Enter Bills" from the "Vendors" menu.

3. Choose the "Credit" radio button to record the return of items.

4. Enter the vendor's name.

5. Under the "Items" tab, enter the same amounts as the reimbursement check for the returned products.

6. Click "Save & Close."

Linking the Deposit to the Bill Credit:

1. Choose "Pay Bills" from the "Vendors" menu.

2. Ensure that the deposit amount matches the vendor check.

3. Apply the Bill Credit you created earlier by selecting "Set Credits," then click "Done."

4. After selecting "Pay Selected Bills," click "Done" once again.

For Vendor Refunds as Credit Card Credits:

1. Select "Enter Credit Card Charges" from the "Banking" menu.

2. Choose the credit card account from the "Credit Card" drop-down menu.

3. Select "Refund/Credit" from the radio buttons.

4. Enter the date, reference number, and amount after selecting the appropriate vendor name.

5. Provide an explanatory memo for the transaction.

6. Under the "Item" tab, input the items and refund amounts if any items are returned.

7. Under the "Expenses" tab, choose the appropriate accounts, then input the amount if the refund doesn't include any items.

8. Click "Save & Close."

Managing Recurring Transactions

If you've set up recurring transactions to automate regular purchases and expenses, such as monthly rent, follow these steps to view all your recurring transactions in one place:

1. Go to "Reports" from the "Business overview" menu or access reports directly.

2. Open the "Recurring Template List" report.

3. Customize the report as needed.

4. In the "Filter" section, select the "Distribution Account" checkbox and choose specific accounts from the dropdown.

5. Click "Run report."

This report displays your recurring transaction templates along with their associated accounts, amounts, and quantities. Managing your finances and recurring transactions is essential for running a successful business.

CHAPTER 6

A Guide to Paying Employees and Contractors

Choosing between hiring someone as an employee or an independent contractor is a significant decision with implications for taxes, payroll requirements, and more. While there are numerous laws governing this distinction, here's a brief overview and a list of helpful resources to consider.

An employee is an individual hired by an employer, typically subject to more employer control.

In contrast, an independent contractor is a self-employed individual who provides services to businesses under their own terms.

If you classify someone as an employee, you must:

1. Withhold and remit payroll taxes, including income, Social Security, and Medicare taxes.

2. Contribute the same amount of Social Security and Medicare taxes as the employee.

3. Pay federal and state unemployment taxes on employee earnings.

4. Issue a Form W-2 at the end of the year.

For self-employed individuals:

1. Payroll taxes are not withheld.

2. Federal and state unemployment taxes are not your responsibility.

3. A 1099-MISC form should be provided each year.

Getting Started with QuickBooks Payroll

QuickBooks Online Payroll offers automation, reliability, and flexibility for managing payroll. This allows you to focus on providing financial guidance to your clients and expanding your business, all while ensuring that their payroll needs are handled efficiently.

You can manage payroll, access health benefits, and provide HR support for your clients through QuickBooks Online Payroll. QuickBooks Time, which integrates accounting, payroll, and time tracking, streamlines business administration.

Key features of QuickBooks Payroll:

- Automated payroll operation

- Pay W2s and 1099 contractors in a single transaction

- Seamless integration of automated timekeeping with QuickBooks Online Payroll

- Automatic calculation, filing, and payment of payroll taxes on both federal and state levels

- Clear notifications and messages to keep you in control

Enabling QuickBooks Payroll:

Upon logging into your new QuickBooks Online Payroll account, a popup will appear to accept the New Pricing and Billing Terms and Conditions. Accept these terms to ensure uninterrupted payroll processing.

In your toolbar navigation, you can use the following icons:

- Search: Easily search for specific employees or payroll transactions without navigating through menus.

- Notifications: Access important reminders and alerts regarding tax dates, product news, and more.

- Settings: Configure your payroll preferences, manage users, and change companies within this section.

To update your payroll accounting preferences, follow these steps:

1. Log in as the Primary Admin in QuickBooks Online.

2. Click "Account and settings" under Settings.

3. Choose "Billing & Subscription."

4. Review your payroll plan details, and ensure the configuration suits your needs.

You have flexibility in the order in which you complete these tasks, and the configuration is designed to allow you to enter information at your convenience and save it as you go.

If you've already paid your employees this year, there are additional tasks to perform, which can be accessed through the "Overview" section.

To manage your payroll accounting settings, follow these steps:

Step 1: Determine the account type for your payroll transactions.

- Your payroll liabilities and costs are recorded in default accounts automatically generated by QuickBooks Online Payroll.

- However, you can create new accounts within your QuickBooks Online Chart of Accounts to separately track payroll expenses and deductions.

- Be aware that QuickBooks doesn't allow using a different account type, such as cost of goods sold, for payroll expenses and liabilities.

Step 2: Add or edit your payroll account register.

- Edit the current account if you want to change its type or name.

- Add a new account if you want to use a different account for specific payroll items.

- Instructions for adding or changing a payroll account are provided.

Step 3: Update your payroll accounting preferences.

- Access Payroll settings from the Settings menu.

- Choose "Edit" when "Accounting" is selected.

- Update specific sections as needed.

- Select the account where the transaction for each payroll item should be recorded, then click "Continue."

For changes to past transactions, choose "Edit" and specify a start date. You can modify accounts for each section, except for the Bank Account section.

Setting up Payroll Taxes

Determining the state payroll taxes that apply to you and your employees depends on their place of residence and work. These taxes may include local taxes, state disability insurance, state unemployment insurance, and paid family leave. To add a new state to your payroll product when you have an employee in that state, follow these steps:

Step 1: Identify Applicable State Taxes and Gather Information

Calculating the correct state and municipal taxes can be complex, as each situation is unique.

Contact the state withholding and unemployment insurance offices, along with any relevant municipal tax offices in the areas where your employees reside and work.

These agencies can help determine the applicable taxes for your situation and provide you with the necessary account numbers to file and pay taxes.

To set up the new state in your payroll product, you will need the following information based on the state taxes that apply:

- Account number(s)

- Frequency of tax payments

- Tax rates

Handling Roaming Employees

If your employees work in multiple states during a specific period, they may be required to pay State Unemployment Insurance (SUI) or local taxes in each state where they work.

Keep in mind that our payroll tools can handle only one SUI tax or local tax jurisdiction per employee, and we recommend avoiding workarounds that may complicate state tax forms.

Step 2: Set Up or Modify Your Employees

After determining the state or local taxes you need to file and pay, you can add new employees or make changes to existing ones.

Step 3: Set Up Your New State Taxes

If you want to file your forms and pay your taxes electronically, you must complete the state tax setup. Account numbers are not required to set up state taxes, but you'll need to manually file the paperwork and make tax payments until the account numbers are entered.

Step 4: Sign New State Authorization Forms

Depending on your payroll service, you may be required to sign authorization forms before we can file your paperwork and pay your state taxes.

Preparing Payroll

Step 1: Navigate to Payroll

After signing in to your QuickBooks account, go to the "Payroll" tab to get started. If you've recently purchased a QuickBooks Online subscription, you'll find a "Get Started" button. Click it to proceed to the next screen, where you'll be asked a few questions to determine your payroll needs.

Step 2: Enter General Information About Paying Your Employees

The system will ask if you've already paid employees for the current calendar year. Select "Yes" if you're transitioning from a manual system or another payroll program to QuickBooks Payroll.

You'll also need to provide year-to-date (YTD) payroll information and tax payments made for each employee.

Step 3: Add Employees

Upon entering your workplace, a new window will open for entering basic personnel data and payroll information.

Click the "Add an employee" button to start entering information for each employee on your payroll.

Step 4: Complete Employee Information

To set up QuickBooks Online Payroll, you'll need to provide the following information for each employee:

- Pay schedule

- Employee pay

- Employee deductions/contributions

- Employee withholding information

- YTD payroll information

- Payment method

Step 5: Click on "Run Payroll"

Access your "Payroll" dashboard and click the "Run Payroll" button in the top right corner.

Step 6: Enter Current Hours

For salaried employees, the system will automatically fill in the total hours based on the preset amount of work hours during initial setup. However, you must manually enter the actual working hours for hourly employees in the "Regular Pay Hrs" column.

Step 7: Review and Submit Payroll

Review your employees' payment method, the number of hours worked, and other payment details, as well as employee and employer tax contributions.

Click "Preview payroll" to check the data. If everything is correct, click "Submit Payroll." Afterward, you can print payroll checks and direct deposit remittance advice, and bills will be generated if you use QuickBooks Online as your accounting program for easy reconciliation.

Enabling Employee Time Tracking

To use the employee time tracking feature for keeping tabs on project or activity hours and billing clients, follow these steps:

1. Navigate to Account and settings under Settings.

2. Choose the Time tab.

3. Select Edit in the General or Timesheet section.

4. Configure your time tracking preferences, including:

- First day of the work week: Affecting how employees and contractors see weekly timesheets.

- Show service field: Allowing employees and contractors to indicate services performed.

- Make time billable: Allowing employees and contractors to specify billable activities.

- Show billing rate to users entering time (optional).

5. Click Save and Done.

With these settings in place, you can now add a time tracking user:

1. Choose Manage users under Settings.

2. Select Add user.

3. Choose Only Time tracking.

4. Click Next.

5. Locate the worker or vendor you wish to add, click Next, and fill out their contact information.

6. Choose Save.

Note that the user type for a Time Tracking Only user cannot be changed. If you require different corporate access for a time tracker, remove the user and re-add them with the new user type.

Reviewing and Generating Payroll Checks

Even if you use another service for payroll in addition to QuickBooks for accounting, you must continue to track those paychecks in QuickBooks to keep all your payroll and account information in one place. Here's how to do it:

Step 1: Create Manual Tracking Accounts

If you haven't already, add additional accounts to your Chart of Accounts for tracking your payroll liabilities and expenses. Create the following expense accounts with the account type "Expense":

- Payroll Expenses: Wages

- Payroll Expenses: Taxes

Step 2: Insert Payroll Paychecks into QuickBooks Online

After paying your staff outside of QuickBooks, create a journal entry for each paycheck. You can obtain payroll reports or pay stubs from your payroll service to enter the data into QuickBooks.

Follow these steps:

1. Choose + New.

2. Select Journal Entry.

3. Enter the paycheck date.

4. If you want, enter the paycheck number.

5. Create the journal entry using the data from your paycheck report.

You can combine the paycheck totals for any employees paid during the pay period into a single journal entry or write separate entries for each employee if needed.

Setting Up or Correcting Payroll Exemptions

QuickBooks Online Payroll Core, Premium, and Elite allow you to adjust previous payrolls.

Depending on how employees were paid and system restrictions, you may be able to void, edit, or delete a paycheck. Follow these steps:

1. Locate the Paycheck list page.

2. Navigate to the specific paycheck you want to correct.

3. Click the down arrow on the right of that row.

The system will recalculate your taxes and make necessary adjustments with the next payroll run after you make a correction.

Printing Payroll Reports

To print payroll reports in QuickBooks, follow these steps:

- Ensure the payroll report you want to print is accessible.

- Select Share.

- Choose the printing options for your report:

- Export to Excel: If you want to print your report as an Excel document.

- Printer Friendly: Select this option, then choose Print to print your report as it appears in your payroll account.

Managing Payroll Taxes

When it's time to pay your payroll taxes, QuickBooks Payroll (QP) guides you on the amount due and helps you create the necessary payroll tax documents for submission to the relevant revenue agency.

Paying Payroll Taxes

To pay your payroll taxes using QuickBooks Payroll:

- Access Payroll Tax under Taxes and click Pay Taxes.

- You will see all unpaid taxes listed.

- To record a payment for a tax item, click Record Payment next to the tax item.

- After reviewing the data on the following screen, select Record and print.

Viewing Payroll Tax Forms

To view payroll tax forms in QuickBooks Payroll:

- Go to Payroll Tax under Taxes.

- Choose Monthly, Annual, or Employer Forms from the Forms section.

- You can generate quarterly or monthly tax forms and worksheets for monthly forms (e.g., PD7A).

- For Annual Forms, you can create T4s and the T4 Summary report.

- Employer Forms allow you to construct Records of Employment (ROE).

Paying Contractors

Independent contractors are self-employed individuals who provide services to businesses.

Here's how to set up 1099-eligible contractors in QuickBooks:

Add a Contractor as a Vendor

1. Select Contractors under Payroll.

2. Click on Add a contractor.

3. Enter the contractor's information or use the "Email this contractor" button to have them complete it.

4. After filling in the details, choose Add contractor.

Track Contractor Payments for 1099s

Once you've added a contractor as a vendor, you should begin tracking their payments. Follow these steps:

1. Click on Sales or Get paid & pay, then select Vendors.

2. Open the profile of the vendor you want to track.

3. Choose Edit.

4. Check the Track Payments for 1099 checkbox.

Reporting on 1099 Vendor Payments

To prepare for 1099 filings, you can use QuickBooks reports to determine who needs to have 1099s filed for them.

Here's how to run these reports:

See All 1099 Vendors

1. Select Reports from the Business Overview menu or click Report and look for the Vendor Contact List option.

2. Choose Customize.

3. Select Change columns under Rows/Columns.

4. Check the box next to Track 1099.

5. Click on Run Report.

To See 1099 Totals, Accounts, and More

1. Select Reports from the Business Overview menu or navigate to Reports.

2. Enter "1099 Transaction Detail Report," "1099 Contractor Balance Detail," or "1099 Contractor Balance Summary" in the search bar.

To See All Payments to Vendors Requiring 1099s

1. Select Expenses under Transactions, under Bookkeeping, or directly under Expenses.

2. Choose Contractors after selecting Vendors or Payroll.

3. Once you reach the "Check that the payments add up" window, click Prepare 1099, and then select Continue.

4. By choosing the arrow next to the filter icon at the top of the table, you can determine which contractors are eligible for 1099.

Preparing 1099 Forms

QuickBooks Online offers a time-saving feature that allows you to generate your 1099 forms using the data already stored in your accounts.

When you make payments to contractors, it's essential to file tax paperwork known as 1099s with the IRS.

Here's how you can create your 1099s (1099-MISC and 1099-NEC) in QuickBooks Online:

1. Access Contractors or Vendors under Payroll or Get paid & pay.

2. Choose Let's get started, and then select Prepare 1099s.

3. Verify that your company's name, address, and tax ID match the information on tax notices or letters from the IRS.

4. Next, select the boxes that correspond to the types of payments made to your contractors during the year. It's crucial to choose these boxes carefully because there have been updates to the 1099 forms. Most businesses will select "Non-employee compensation (Box 1 1099-NEC)."

However, if you believe you made other types of payments, consult with your accountant.

5. Ensure all your contractors are listed, and their contact information, including email addresses, is accurate.

6. Review the payment totals for each box chosen in step 4. The 1099-NEC and 1099-MISC forms will automatically receive the respective payment details. Select Next.

- Note: Electronic payments made to contractors (e.g., by credit card) won't appear in this list because the credit card company, bank, etc., reports them on your behalf.

You can verify these payments by checking the year and threshold directly above the Name column if needed.

7. Choose E-File if you want QuickBooks to e-file your 1099s, or select I'll file myself if you prefer to print and mail the forms independently.

For a business to thrive, it must rely on employees in various roles and occasionally hire contractors for their services. QuickBooks Online makes it easy to manage payments to these individuals.

CHAPTER 7

Managing Bank and Credit Card Accounts

Adding a bank account for handling expenses is a straightforward process. We demonstrate two methods for setting up your bank account in QuickBooks Online: instant validation and manual entry.

Creating a New Bank Account

To establish a new bank account, follow these steps:

1. Log in to your QuickBooks Online account.

2. Select "Account and settings" under the "Settings" menu.

3. Choose "Bill Pay."

4. Decide on a bank account.

5. Opt to create a new bank account.

Recording a Bank Deposit

We guide you on how to record client payments and recommend using the "Undeposited Funds" account when entering a "Receive Payment" transaction. This keeps your actual bank account unchanged until you're ready to make a bank deposit.

The update happens when you're prepared to create a bank deposit.

When reconciling your bank statement, it's important to compare the bank's deposits and withdrawals with your recorded deposits and withdrawals.

If you record each customer payment as a direct deposit in your bank account, it may not match the bank's representation. However, depositing client payments into the "Undeposited Funds" account allows for a more accurate reconciliation because you can consolidate multiple checks from that account into your bank account as a single deposit.

Follow these steps to create a bank deposit:

1. Select "Bank Deposit" from the "Create" menu by clicking the Create button with the plus (+) sign. QuickBooks Online opens the "Bank Deposit" transaction window.

2. In the "Select the Payments Included in This Deposit" section at the top of the window, you'll find existing payment transactions. Add any additional payment transactions not associated with an open invoice using the lines in the "Add Funds to This Deposit" section.

3. Choose the account where you wish to deposit the payments at the top of the window.

4. Check the box next to each transaction you want to include in the deposit in the "Select the Payments Included in This Deposit" section.

5. Indicate the payment method for each transaction you intend to deposit.

6. Optionally, provide a memo and reference number. The total amount of the selected payments and the deposit amount will be displayed below the "Choose the Payments Included in This Deposit" list, unless you add items to the "Add Funds to This Deposit" section.

7. Scroll down in the "Bank Deposit" transaction window. Adding a memo for the deposit is optional. Optionally, include a cash return amount, which represents the portion of the deposit total you don't intend to deposit, along with the account where it should be placed and a note explaining its intended use.

8. Finally, click "Save and Close."

Managing Bank and Credit Card Transactions

Handling Credit Card Paymen

To process credit cards in QuickBooks Online, you need a QuickBooks Payments account.

Even if you don't use QuickBooks Payments, it's essential to enter credit card payments made outside of QuickBooks. Make sure to create an account with QuickBooks Payments before proceeding.

Before you continue, ensure the following:

- Create an account with QuickBooks Payments.

- Determine where you want to track your fees and payments.

You can use your payments account for processing card payments in two ways, depending on whether you use QuickBooks to create invoices.

Option 1: Receiving Payment for an Invoice

If you invoice your clients and wish to receive payments, you can apply payments to open invoices:

1. Select "+ New."

2. Choose either "Receive payment" or "Receive payment on an invoice."

3. Enter the customer's information and payment due date.

4. In the "Outstanding Transactions" section, select an open invoice to apply the payment. You can enter a different amount in the "Amount Received" column for partial payments.

5. Choose "Credit card" from the payment method dropdown.

6. Select "Enter credit card information."

7. Opt to "Swipe Card" or manually enter the credit card details.

8. If you want to save the customer's credit card information for future transactions, choose "Use this credit card in the future."

9. Enter the credit card details.

10. Choose "Save" and then select "Save and new" or "Save and close."

Option 2: Crediting a Sales Receipt

If you do not invoice your clients and instead use sales receipts, follow these steps:

1. Choose "+ New."

2. After selecting "Sales receipt" or "Make a sale," fill in the customer information.

3. Add a product or service to the sale.

4. Choose "Credit card" from the payment method dropdown.

5. Select "Enter credit card information."

6. Opt to "Swipe Card" or manually enter the credit card details.

7. If you want to save the customer's credit card information for future transactions, choose "Use this credit card in the future."

8. Enter the credit card details.

9. Choose "Save" and then select "Save and new" or "Save and close."

Recording a Credit Card Credit

To add a credit card credit in QuickBooks Online, follow these steps:

1. Click "+ New" in the Navigation Bar.

2. Click "Credit Card Credit" in the menu under the "Vendors" title, and the "Credit Card Credit" window will appear.

3. Choose the merchant from which you made the purchase using the Payee dropdown.

4. Select the credit card you used from the Bank/Credit account dropdown.

5. Enter the appropriate Category or Item details based on the account or items for which you are receiving credit. Ensure these details match the initial transaction or bill paid with the credit card.

6. Click "Save and close" to save the credit card information and exit the page. Alternatively, you can select "Save and new" from the dropdown menu to save the current transaction and open a new, empty "Credit Card Credit" window.

Reconciling Bank or Credit Card Accounts

Reconciliation is the process of ensuring that your QuickBooks transactions align with your bank and credit card statements.

Just like balancing your checkbook, this ensures the accuracy of your accounts.

Follow these steps to reconcile your accounts:

1. Review your opening balance, especially if you're reconciling an account for the first time. It should match your actual bank account balance when you started using QuickBooks.

2. Begin reconciliation once you have your monthly bank or credit card statement. Reconcile statements one at a time, starting with the oldest.

3. If your accounts are linked to online banking, categorize and match each downloaded transaction.

4. In QuickBooks Online, access "Reconcile" under "Settings." If you're reconciling for the first time, select "Get started."

5. Choose the account you want to reconcile from the Account menu, ensuring it matches the one on your statement.

6. Verify that the Starting balance matches the statement's beginning balance.

7. Enter the Ending balance and Ending date from your statement.

8. Review the Last statement ending date, which indicates the end date of your most recent reconciliation.

9. Select "Start Reconciliation" when you're ready.

10. Compare your statement's transactions with those in QuickBooks. Check each transaction separately, ensuring the dates and transactions match.

For accounts connected to online banking, reconciliation is typically straightforward as your bank provides transaction details.

For non-connected accounts, you'll need to manually compare transactions and ensure the difference between your statement and QuickBooks is $0.00.

Balancing your bank and credit card accounts is a crucial part of maintaining financial accuracy in your business.

Streamlining Bank and Credit Card Transactions

Syncing with Financial Institutions

QuickBooks offers a powerful feature known as online banking, or "bank feeds," to simplify your financial management.

This unique function allows you to effortlessly connect your bank accounts, credit cards, and other financial institutions to your QuickBooks Online account.

By doing so, you eliminate the need for manual data entry and save valuable time. With the assistance of our outsourced accountants, you can seamlessly integrate QuickBooks with your online bank account.

Once your financial accounts are linked to your QuickBooks Online account, all transactions conducted through those accounts are automatically downloaded and categorized by QuickBooks.

After reviewing and approving QuickBooks' categorization, you can easily access your updated credit card transactions, sales records, and expenses.

Connecting QuickBooks Accounts to Financial Institutions

1. Access QuickBooks Online.

2. If you haven't created an account, choose "Connect" from the banking option on the landing page. If you already have an account, select "Add Account."

3. Search for your bank on the list (most banks, even small credit unions, can be connected). If your bank isn't listed but you still want

to add your transactions to QuickBooks, you can manually upload a CSV file.

4. After clicking "Continue," enter your online banking login information in the pop-up box and click "Connect." The time required to link your bank account to QuickBooks online can vary, and certain banks may request additional security information, in which case on-screen instructions will guide you.

When you want to re-connect QuickBooks Online to your bank account, follow these steps:

1. Go to "Banking" and select "Banking" at the top.

2. After clicking "Add Account," enter your bank's name.

3. Choose the bank with an existing connection if you plan to use the same login information.

4. If you're using different credentials, select the bank with a new connection.

5. After entering your username and password, click "Continue."

6. Select the QuickBooks account and choose the account from your chart of accounts.

7. Once connected, click "I'm done" and then "Connect."

Accessing Bank and Credit Card-Related Pages in QuickBooks

You can significantly reduce the need for manual data entry and expedite transaction categorization by using bank feeds or online banking. Transactions are downloaded and categorized automatically once your accounts are linked—all that's left is your approval.

Directly Connecting a Bank or Credit Card Account

Here's how to connect a bank or credit card account:

1. Navigate to "Banking" or "Bookkeeping," then select "Transactions," and choose "Bank transactions."

2. Opt for "Connect account" if this is your first time setting up a bank account. If you already have an account, choose "Link account." Note: If you're switching from QuickBooks Desktop for security reasons, you must reconnect your bank and credit card accounts.

3. Enter your bank, credit card, or credit union's name in the search area. If your bank isn't listed but you want to add your transactions, you can manually upload them.

4. Choose "Continue" and use your user ID and password to log in to your bank.

5. Follow the on-screen steps, which may include security checks required by your bank. The connection may take a moment.

6. Select the accounts you want to link and pick an account type that matches your chart of accounts in QuickBooks.

7. Choose how many transactions you wish to download in the past. Some banks provide up to 90 days' worth of transactions, while others go back up to 24 months.

8. Select "Connect."

Managing Uploaded or Downloaded Activity

QuickBooks immediately downloads the latest transactions from your bank and credit card accounts after linking them. It searches for matches with transactions already in QuickBooks, creating new transaction records when necessary. You need only approve the matches or newly created transactions.

Downloading the Latest Bank and Credit Card Transactions

Most banks have their transactions downloaded to QuickBooks around 10 PM PT daily. Some banks may take longer. If you want the most recent transactions immediately, you can manually update your accounts:

1. Select "Bank transactions" under "Bookkeeping," "Transactions," or "Banking."

2. Choose "Update."

Reviewing Transactions

To review transactions in detail:

1. Go to "Banking" or "Bookkeeping," then click "Transactions," and select "Bank transactions."

2. Choose the account you want to review.

3. Click "For review" to begin your review. The "For review" tab contains downloaded transactions sent by QuickBooks for your review.

Automating Downloaded Activity with Rules

Use bank rules to expedite the processing of transactions from bank feeds. These rules analyze downloaded transactions for specific information and assign particular payees and categories accordingly. You can create, replicate, delete, or amend rules on the bank transactions page.

To create a rule:

1. Click "Banking" in the Navigation pane.

2. Choose "Bank rules" at the top of the list of bank and credit cards.

3. Select the "New Rule" button in the upper right corner.

4. Name the rule.

5. Choose the accounts to which the rule should apply, specifying whether it relates to money in or out of QuickBooks.

6. Set criteria for QuickBooks to use when determining whether the rule applies to downloaded transactions.

7. Specify the data that QuickBooks should apply to transactions meeting the rule's requirements. This includes transaction type, payee, categories, memo, and the option to automatically add transactions to your books.

8. Click "Save."

With these rules, you can efficiently manage your bank and credit card transactions, reducing the need for manual data entry and enhancing your financial management within QuickBooks.

Correcting Errors in Uploaded or Downloaded Transactions

QuickBooks Online (QBO) makes it easy to identify and rectify errors in transactions, whether they were manually entered or automatically applied by rules.

Here's how to fix mistakes:

1. Distinguish Transactions: On the Bank and Credit Cards page, QBO differentiates between transactions entered manually and those added automatically by rules using distinct icons in the Category or Match column. This helps you quickly identify transactions to which QBO has applied rules.

2. Review Transactions: Utilize the "Reviewed" option on the Bank and Credit Cards page to assess how QBO manages each downloaded transaction in your business.

3. Correcting Mistakes: If you accidentally included a transaction in QBO that should not be there or if QBO misclassified a transaction, you can easily fix these errors using the "In QuickBooks" tab on the Bank and Credit Cards page.

4. Undo a Transaction: To reverse a transaction added in error or corrected incorrectly, follow these steps:

a. Locate Transaction: On the Bank and Credit Cards page, select the "Reviewed" option.

b. Undo Transaction: In the Action column, find the transaction you want to undo, and then click the "Undo" button. QBO will confirm the successful reversal.

c. Review and Accept: Move to the "For Review" tab, locate the transaction, make the necessary adjustments, and re-accept it. If needed, you can also exclude the transaction from QBO.

By following these steps, you can efficiently correct any errors in your uploaded or downloaded transactions within QuickBooks Online.

Managing Connections to Financial Institutions via Indirect Methods

When dealing with financial transactions, QuickBooks offers indirect connections, such as downloading Web Connect and text files, or connecting to online providers through app transactions.

Here's how to utilize these methods effectively:

Downloading Web Connect and Text Files

1. To download transactions as a .QBO file, log in to your bank's website.

2. In QuickBooks Desktop (QBDT), access the File menu.

3. Choose "Web Connect Files" by going through Utilities, Import, and then Utilities.

4. Select "Open" after you've chosen the .QBO file you saved.

5. Pick the appropriate bank account.

6. Click "Next."

7. QuickBooks will read the data successfully, and you'll receive a confirmation dialogue. Click "OK."

8. Head to the Bank Feeds Center for further management.

Opening Text Files in Microsoft Excel or Google Sheets

You can also open a text file in Excel as an Excel workbook. Here's how:

1. Navigate to the location of the text file: File > Open.

2. In the Open dialog box, select "Text Files" from the file type dropdown menu.

3. Locate the text file and double-click it.

- For .txt files, Excel launches the Import Text Wizard. Click "Finish" to complete the import process.

- If the file is in .csv format, Excel opens it and presents the data in a new worksheet.

Saving CSV Files

If you want to save a worksheet as a text file, follow these steps:

1. Select "Save As" under the File menu.

2. Choose "Text or CSV" from the "Save as type" dropdown in the Save As dialog box.

3. Select "Save" after specifying the location for the new text file.

- If saving in CSV format, you might receive a warning about potential loss of functionality.

Uploading Web Connect and CSV Files

To upload the downloaded files, follow these steps:

1. Navigate to Banking or Bookkeeping, then click "Transactions," and then "Bank Transactions."

2. Choose the blue tile for the account containing the transactions you want to submit.

3. From the drop-down menu next to "Link account," choose "Upload from file."

4. Select the file you downloaded from your bank, either by dragging and dropping or through file selection. Then, click "Continue."

5. Choose the QuickBooks account you want to upload the transactions into and click "Continue."

6. Follow the onscreen instructions to match the columns on the file with the appropriate fields in QuickBooks. Then, click "Continue."

7. Select the transactions you want to import and click "Continue."

8. Confirm by clicking "Yes."

9. Click "Done" once you've reviewed and approved the transactions.

Connecting to Online Providers Through App Transactions

You can manage transactions from online providers, such as PayPal, using the Connect to PayPal app.

Here's how to set it up:

1. Log in to your QuickBooks Online account.

2. Go to "Apps" and select "Find Apps."

3. Search for "Connect to PayPal."

4. Choose "Get the app now."

5. Install the app by checking the box next to the relevant file and selecting "Let's do it."

6. Provide authorization for Intuit to retrieve data from your PayPal account.

7. Enter the email associated with your PayPal account and follow the instructions based on your account status.

8. Register for a PayPal account if you don't have one.

9. Select "Agree and Connect" to complete the sync after choosing your PayPal bank and sales tax rate.

10. If you have historical transactions, choose the desired import date and click "Done."

By following these steps, you can effectively manage your connections to financial institutions through indirect methods in QuickBooks.

Leveraging QuickBooks Reports for Informed Business Decisions

Reports are invaluable tools for assessing your company's financial health in QuickBooks Online (QBO).

They provide a snapshot of your business performance and can be customized to suit your specific needs. Let's explore how to navigate the Reports section efficiently.

Exploring the Reports Page

The Reports page in QBO provides a plethora of report options to choose from, helping you gauge your business's performance. The reports are categorized for easy access, and they can be found under the following groups:

- Favorites

- Business Overview

- Who Owes You

- Sales and Customers

- What You Owe

- Expenses and Vendors

- Sales Tax

- Employees

- For My Accountant

- Payroll

The availability of payroll reports depends on your subscription. If you don't have a payroll subscription, you'll have limited access to payroll-related reports.

Finding Your Desired Report

Reports in QBO are divided into three categories:

1. Standard Reports: These reports are based on your QBO subscription, usage, preferences, and any add-ons you have installed. To make your most-used reports easily accessible, you can mark them as favorites by clicking the star icon. Starred reports appear at the top of the "Favorites" section in the Standard tab.

2. Custom Reports: The Custom Reports tab lists any reports you've customized and saved, either as individual reports or within report groups.

3. Management Reports: On the Management Reports tab, you can generate predefined report packages, which include several related reports, a table of contents, and a cover page. This feature is particularly handy for assessing overall business performance.

Management reports can be viewed and printed in PDF format.

Searching for a Specific Report

To find a specific report quickly, you don't have to navigate through the tabs.

You can use the "Find a Report by Name" search box in the top right corner of the Reports page. Enter the report name or relevant keywords, and QBO will provide a dropdown list of reports matching your criteria. Click on the desired report to view it.

Additionally, you can use the Search button located at the top of the QBO screen, next to the Gear menu, to search for reports regardless of the page you're on.

Printing a Report

To generate and view a report:

1. Click on the title of the report.

2. QBO will display the report using default settings.

3. If you need to review the details underneath the figures, you can drill down by selecting specific account amounts, allowing you to see the contributing transactions. For instance, in a Profit and Loss report, you can choose an Income or Expense account amount to view the underlying transactions.

4. If you wish to maintain the original summary version of the report while viewing the details, duplicate the tab in your browser.

- In Chrome, right-click a tab and choose "Duplicate" from the context menu.

- In Firefox, right-click the tab and select "Replicate tab" from the context menu.

5. You can close the tab containing the details when you're done.

In summary, QuickBooks reports offer a comprehensive view of your company's financial health, helping you make informed decisions.

Whether you need to assess your business overview, track sales, manage expenses, or generate payroll reports, QuickBooks Reports have you covered.

Utilize the search function to quickly locate specific reports, and don't forget to customize reports and mark your favorites for easy access.

Exporting Reports and Data from QuickBooks Online

QuickBooks Online offers various methods for exporting your reports and data, making it easy to save your information for local storage or further analysis.

Here's how to export reports and data:

Exporting to Excel

1. From the toolbar, click on the Settings icon.

2. Go to "Tools" and select "Export Data."

3. On the "Reports" tab, set your desired date range.

4. Use the slider to add or remove items from the "Reports" and "Lists" tabs.

5. Click on "Excel Export."

This process allows you to export multiple reports and lists into separate Excel files, compressed into a zip format for convenience.

Exporting to Google Sheets

1. Open your QuickBooks Online account and log in.

2. Navigate to "Reports" under "Business Overview" in the left navigation panel.

3. Open the report you want to export to Google Sheets.

4. From the "Export" drop-down menu, select "Google Sheets export."

5. Provide the required verification if prompted, which will open your Google account.

6. If necessary, log into your Google account.

QuickBooks Online allows you to seamlessly connect with Google Sheets for efficient data export and analysis.

Custom Reporting with Spreadsheet Sync

With Spreadsheet Sync, you gain the ability to create and customize reports for QuickBooks Online. Please note that pivot tables are not part of this feature.

Here are some additional options:

- Download transaction or account data from QuickBooks Online Advanced into a data table.

- These tables and reports are categorized, facilitating organized data management and customized reporting.

These export options provide flexibility and convenience for managing your financial data, whether you need to analyze it in Excel, Google Sheets, or other external tools.

Automating Data Transformation with Power Query

Introducing Power Query

Power Query is a robust data preparation and transformation tool that simplifies the process of refining and transforming data. It offers both a Power Query Editor for implementing data transformations and a user-friendly graphical interface for accessing data from various sources. T

he location where your data will be stored depends on the software or service utilizing Power Query since it's integrated into many different products.

Power Query enables you to perform Extract, Transform, and Load (ETL) operations, ensuring your data is in the desired format for analysis.

Connecting to QuickBooks Reports

To connect to QuickBooks reports using Power Query, follow these steps:

1. In the API Server administrative console, select "Settings" -> "Connections," and add a new connection after deploying the API Server and ADO.NET Provider for QuickBooks.

2. Provide the necessary authentication values and other connection properties to connect to QuickBooks.

3. You won't need to set specific connection properties when connecting to a local QuickBooks instance.

4. Requests to QuickBooks are made through the Remote Connector, which employs a small embedded web server to accept connections. It also supports SSL/TLS for secure connections from remote machines.

5. Set up the API Server to use an OData protocol version compatible with Power Query. Navigate to "Settings" -> "Server" in the API Server administrative console and set the "Default Version" property to 3.0.

6. In Excel, go to "Power Query" -> "From Other Data Sources" -> "From OData Feed," enter the OData URL, and click "OK."

7. Define authentication credentials and privacy levels in the wizard, select "Basic authentication," input the login information, and proceed.

8. Modify Power Query's authentication method by clicking "Power Query" -> "Data Source Settings" and "Edit Credential" after selecting the OData stream. Set your desired privacy level.

9. Power Query now allows you to access QuickBooks data. Expand the OData feed node in the Navigator, right-click a table, and select "Edit" to access the Query Editor for the table data.

Removing Header Rows

To ignore or eliminate unnecessary header rows from your data in Power Query:

1. In the Power Query Editor, go to the "Home" tab, click "Remove Rows," and select "Remove Top Rows."

2. Specify the number of rows you want to remove from the top and click "OK." The specified rows will be removed from your data.

Promoting Headers

If Power Query doesn't automatically identify headers in your data, you can manually promote headers as follows:

1. First, remove the top rows from the table. Choose "Remove top rows" from the preview window's upper-left corner and specify the number of rows to remove.

2. After removing the rows, Power Query will allow you to manually promote the headers.

Removing Unwanted Columns

To eliminate unwanted columns in Power Query:

1. In the Power Query Editor, select the column you want to remove, then choose "Home" -> "Remove Columns" -> "Remove Columns."

2. You can also select multiple columns using Ctrl + Click or Shift + Click, and then choose to remove the selected columns or eliminate all columns except the chosen one.

Filtering Unnecessary Rows

To remove rows with blank values in Power Query:

1. Launch the Power Query Editor window and choose the column from which you want to remove rows with empty values.

2. Select "Remove Empty" from the column header's dropdown menu to remove entire rows with empty values.

Power Query allows you to fine-tune and clean your data as needed.

Returning Data to Excel

Data transformation is essential to meet your data analysis requirements. You can customize your data in Power Query by removing columns, altering data types, and filtering rows. These transformations are tracked as steps and enable data shaping to achieve the desired format for your reports and dashboards.

Power Query Editor facilitates these actions, ensuring your data is ready for analysis. Your data is transformed, and a query is created to represent the modified data, comprising all the transformations applied to your data connections. Each transformation is automatically executed when you reload the query.

CONCLUSION

In conclusion, this QuickBooks guide for beginners has provided a comprehensive and foundational understanding of QuickBooks, a powerful accounting software.

We've covered various aspects of QuickBooks, from the basics of setting up your account to performing key accounting tasks efficiently.

Whether you are a small business owner, an aspiring accountant, or someone looking to streamline financial management, this guide has equipped you with the knowledge and tools needed to get started on your QuickBooks journey.

Throughout this guide, you've learned how to:

1. Set Up Your QuickBooks Account: We started by guiding you through the process of creating your QuickBooks account, whether it's QuickBooks Online or QuickBooks Desktop.

2. Navigating QuickBooks: You've become familiar with the QuickBooks user interface, understanding how to access the key features and functions.

3. Managing Company Information: We covered essential tasks like setting up your company profile, managing users, and configuring preferences to tailor QuickBooks to your specific needs.

4. Recording Financial Transactions: You've gained insights into the fundamental accounting tasks such as creating invoices, entering bills, and reconciling bank accounts.

5. Tracking Income and Expenses: You've learned how to monitor your financial health by tracking income, expenses, and generating essential reports like profit and loss statements.

6. Inventory and Payroll Management: We introduced you to inventory management and provided an overview of how QuickBooks can assist you in managing payroll.

7. Customizing QuickBooks: You've learned how to customize QuickBooks to meet your unique business requirements, including creating custom fields and reports.

8. Troubleshooting Common Issues: We've discussed some common problems users may encounter and provided tips for resolving them.

9. Advanced Features: While this guide primarily focused on the basics, you now have a foundation to explore more advanced features such as budgeting, forecasting, and advanced reporting.

10. QuickBooks Tips and Best Practices: Throughout the guide, you've received valuable tips and best practices to make your experience with QuickBooks smoother and more efficient.

It's important to remember that QuickBooks is a versatile tool that can adapt to various industries and business sizes. This guide serves as a solid introduction, but there's always more to explore and learn as you delve deeper into your financial management needs.

As you continue your journey with QuickBooks, don't hesitate to explore additional resources, engage in tutorials, and seek assistance from QuickBooks support. Your ability to effectively manage your finances and make informed business decisions will only improve with time and experience.

QuickBooks is not just accounting software; it's a partner in your financial success. With the knowledge gained from this guide and a commitment to learning and growing, you are well on your way to becoming a proficient QuickBooks user.

Whether you are a small business owner, an accountant, or anyone looking to manage finances efficiently, QuickBooks empowers you to make informed decisions and pave the way for financial success.

Happy Bookkeeping and Record Keeping...

Thank you for choosing us! Your purchase is greatly appreciated, and we hope this book satisfies you perfectly.

If you have any questions or need assistance, please don't hesitate to reach out via robertlewistechie@gmail.com